Finding Runaways and Missing Adults

Finding Runaways and Missing Adults:

When No One Else Is Looking

Robert L. Snow

ROWMAN & LITTLEFIELD PUBLISHERS, INC.
Lanham • Boulder • New York • Toronto • Plymouth, UK

Published in the United States of America
by Rowman & Littlefield Publishers, Inc.
A Member of the Rowman & Littlefield Publishing Group
4501 Forbes Boulevard, Suite 200, Lanham, Maryland 20706
www.rowman.com

10 Thornbury Road, Plymouth PL6 7PP United Kingdom

British Library Cataloguing in Publication Information Available

Library of Congress Cataloging-in-Publication Data
Snow, Robert L.
   Finding runaways and missing adults : when no one else is looking / Robert L.
Snow.
      p. cm.
   Includes bibliographical references.
   ISBN 978-1-4422-1062-2 (cloth : alk. paper) — ISBN 978-1-4422-1064-6
(electronic)
   1. Runaway children—United States. 2. Runaway teenagers—United States.
   3. Missing persons—United States. 4. Missing persons—Investigation—United
States. I. Title.
   HV741.S58 2012
   362.74—dc23
                              2011051616

♾™ The paper used in this publication meets the minimum requirements of
American National Standard for Information Sciences—Permanence of Paper
for Printed Library Materials, ANSI/NISO Z39.48-1992.

Printed in the United States of America

This book is dedicated to:
Matt, Stephanie, Rachel, and Sam

And to:
Tony, Alexis, Luke, and Cole

Contents

• 1 •

The Runaway and Missing
Adult Problem in America

On October 15, 2009, thirteen-year-old Francisco Hernandez Jr. of Brooklyn, New York, ran away from home. After getting into trouble at school and apparently fearing what would happen when his parents found out, Francisco, with a Metrocard and only ten dollars in his pocket, boarded a subway in New York City and disappeared. Francisco reportedly suffers from Asperger's syndrome, which causes him to seek isolation and avoid social interaction. Consequently, his fearful parents knew that he wouldn't be able to speak or interact with anyone on the subway or at any other place he might end up. Also, repeated attempts by his parents and others to reach him on his cell phone failed because the battery had apparently been taken out. For days following his disappearance no one knew what had happened to Francisco.

One can only imagine the anguish Francisco's parents must have gone through, waiting day after day with no news of what had happened to their son. The nights, though, would have been even worse, as his parents would likely lie awake fearing for Francisco's safety, wondering if their son was hungry, cold, frightened, injured, being molested, or perhaps even murdered.

Yet, as bad as the situation was, this was not the first time that Francisco had panicked his parents by running away. As is many times the case with runaways (defined as children under the age of eighteen who have voluntarily left their home or caretaker without permission and with the intent of not returning), Francisco had gone missing before. "He disappeared for five hours and we found him in the train,"

1

said his mother, Marisela Garcia, talking about one of Francisco's earlier disappearances on a subway car.[1]

In Francisco's most recent disappearance, and as is often the case with missing persons, the police and the family didn't agree on the handling of the case. Francisco's parents didn't feel that the police were giving the case the priority it deserved. The police, on the other hand, felt that they were taking the case very seriously, conducting interviews at Francisco's school in Bensonhurst and canvassing the neighborhood where he disappeared.

"We have hundreds of cases open in our Missing Persons Unit at any given time," said Police Commissioner Raymond Kelly, explaining why one case cannot garner all of the unit's time.[2]

Police departments often find that the parents of runaway children will feel bitter and disappointed if the department does not put 100 percent of its available resources into searching for their missing children. Yet, with almost two million children running away from home every year in our country, this simply isn't possible or practical. The police department wouldn't have any manpower left for its other duties. Therefore, to assure the best possible chance of quickly finding runaway children, parents and other family members mustn't leave the job of looking for these children totally up to the police, but must join in the search themselves. And, as I will show later, family members are often more likely to be successful in their search than the police anyway.

So what happened to Francisco?

For eleven days after disappearing Francisco apparently rode subway trains undetected. He would eat and sleep on the trains, and use the bathrooms in the various stations. This occurred despite the fact that Francisco's family had posted over 2,000 missing person fliers with his picture on them in the subway system and throughout New York City. Even stranger, though, the busy New York City subway has an extensive surveillance system that for some reason didn't flag the lone boy living and sleeping in their train cars for eleven days.

Fortunately, a transit police officer at the Stillwell Avenue Station in Coney Island saw one of the fliers that Francisco's family had posted, and then almost immediately spotted a lone boy sitting in a stopped car of the D Train. The officer asked Francisco if he was the runaway boy on the poster, and Francisco said yes.

"I didn't want anyone to scream at me," Francisco later told the authorities when asked about his reason for running away.[3]

Francisco, the police found, had only thirty cents left and had lived on potato chips, jelly rolls, and other junk food he had purchased with the original ten dollars he carried. The police returned Francisco, unharmed, to his parents.

Fortunately, this case had a happy ending. And even though the family of Francisco had been actively involved in searching for him, was there anything more they could have done that might have sped up the discovery of their missing boy? Yes, there were several things, as we will discuss in a following chapter, that could very likely have turned up Francisco in a much shorter time than eleven days, some that could have done it within minutes of discovering he had disappeared.

This anecdote also illustrates a very important point that I saw many times in my thirty-eight-year career as a police officer: runaway children are seldom running away to better circumstances. Although not so in Francisco's case, even children who run away from homes where the environment is far from perfect, quite often end up in situations much, much worse. Runaway children can, and many times do, fall prey to adults who sexually assault them, who introduce them to dangerous drugs, force them to take part in prostitution and/or pornographic movies, and occasionally lead them to even worse fates. In the case of Francisco, only good fortune spared him from the dangers that can befall many runaway children.

As an example of these dangers, in July 2009, the police in Clearwater, Florida, charged four men with having sex with a twelve-year-old runaway girl. The authorities suspect that even more men will be charged in this case.

In another incident, in September 2006, the police arrested two men for harboring a sixteen-year-old girl who had run away from her home in Ukiah, California. The house the men harbored the girl in, located in Philo, California, about twenty miles southwest of Ukiah, allegedly had a reputation for being a "party and drug house." Because of this, the young girl, when found by the police, turned out to be under the influence of methamphetamines.

In March 2009, a sixteen-year-old girl in Kentucky ran away from home with Ian Nelson, a twenty-seven-year-old man she had met online. Computer chatting is now one of the most popular methods child predators use to find their victims. The police arrested Nelson in the company of the young runaway girl after the pair had traveled together to Aurora, Illinois. The authorities said they planned to charge Nelson with Solicitation of a Minor to Commit Aggravated Statutory Rape.[4]

As a further example of the dangers faced by runaways, in June 2008, the FBI's Crimes against Children Unit announced that it had rescued twenty-one children and arrested 389 adults for trafficking children in prostitution, many of these children being runaways. This was the fifth year of the FBI's Innocence Lost Initiative, which by 2008 had rescued a total of 433 children from prostitution.[5]

"We have to treat those kids as victims," said Seattle police detective Tina Drain about runaway children. "They are not just missing. What they are is vulnerable to predators."[6]

As Detective Drain says, many adults target runaways as easy victims. "With young girls, you promise them heaven, they'll follow you to hell," said the pimp of a female runaway upon his sentencing for pandering the underage girl.[7]

Researchers in several studies have found that the average age of a child first used for prostitution is between eleven and fourteen.[8] And this threat, incidentally, doesn't befall just female runaways. Male runaways can also be forced into this life. In addition to prostitution, though, makers of pornography will often coerce runaways into taking part in their films, occasionally through threats of violence, but more often through promises of money and other resources the runaways need to survive.

Along with prostitution and pornography, illegal drugs loom as a real danger to runaways as well. According to a long-term study from the federal government's Office of Juvenile Justice and Delinquency Prevention, 35 percent of located runaways were either in the company of someone using illegal drugs or were using illegal drugs themselves during their absence from home.[9]

So, even with all of these dangers, how many children run away from home every year in our country? No one really knows the true number. While I noted earlier that there are almost two million runaway children every year, this is just an estimate. The National Runaway Switchboard, a social services resource for runaways, receives well over 100,000 calls each year (receiving 114,097 in 2008).[10] This is a huge number because only a small percentage of runaways use this resource. Actually, it's hard to give an accurate figure for the total number of runaways annually because often families don't report runaways but prefer to handle the situation on their own, fearing the embarrassment of police involvement and the detrimental effect that a police report will have on their children's future. Also, quite often with persistent runaways the children will return home on their own within twenty-four to forty-eight hours, so the police are never notified unless the children remain missing.

However, a number of studies have given estimates of the size of the problem. The most recent and reliable in-depth study of runaways is the *National Incidence Studies of Missing, Abducted, Runaway, and Thrownaway Children* (NISMART), a research project funded by the federal government. This study, published in 2002, estimated that the number of runaways in our country in 1999 was around 1.7 million. Again, this was just an estimate based on the best information available. The NISMART report states that the 95 percent confidence interval for the annual number of runaways in the United States is between 1.4 and 1.9 million. Interestingly, the study also found that almost 70 percent of these runaways are between the ages of fifteen and seventeen and evenly distributed between boys and girls. But more alarming is that 13 percent of these runaways traveled over 100 miles from home, which makes locating them quickly, before they have the chance to travel this distance, even more imperative.

The report goes on to state that of these almost two million annual runaways, parents contacted the police in only a little over 20 percent of the cases.[11] Seldom is this a good idea. Even though parents, in order to achieve the maximum possibility of success, must take an active part in the search for their runaway children, parents must not exclude the possibility of the police encountering their children while on patrol.

The overall goal is to find and return runaway children before harm can befall them, so parents must involve the police.

While Francisco's case above took place in a large city, where the police department had a unit created specifically for the purpose of handling runaways and missing persons, a recent study showed comparable rates of runaway behavior between metropolitan and nonmetropolitan youth.[12] This can be problematic because in many nonmetropolitan areas the police department may not be large enough to justify a missing persons unit, which means that the task of finding a runaway falls to a detective untrained and inexperienced in locating these individuals.

While fortunately for most parents over 75 percent of runaway children return home on their own within a week, this still means that every year hundreds of thousands of runaway children don't return, leaving anguished parents fearing for their safety. And this fear is certainly not unfounded: the landscape for runaway children is filled with danger.

Yet, because the number of annual runways is so huge, and because so many of them return home on their own, police departments can seldom give the runaway problem the really serious attention parents expect. The manpower required to do this would preclude police departments from doing anything else. So, unless parents can show clear evidence that runaway children are in imminent danger, seldom will the police put the huge effort into finding them that parents expect.

The situation is not hopeless, however. As I will show later in this book, parents and family members are better positioned than anyone else to locate their runaway children, or to locate clues as to their whereabouts. Family members wanting a quick, safe return of runaway children must be willing to do much of the detective work themselves, and in this book I will show readers exactly how to do that.

Also, a possibility that the family members of a suspected runaway child, even a habitual runaway, must also consider is that the child, rather than running away, is missing because he or she has been involved in an accident. This is why it is so important to contact the police.

In addition, there is also the very real possibility that, rather than running away, a child has been abducted. Child abductions can, and do, occur everywhere in America. Around 350,000 take place every year.[13] And while many of these abductions are committed by family members, the overriding motive behind the abduction of young girls by nonfamily members is sexual assault. This is frightening enough, but family members should be particularly aware that when a child is murdered during an abduction, it usually occurs during the first twenty-four to forty-eight hours. Therefore, whether children are actual runaways, have been involved in an accident, or are the victims of an abduction, family members of missing children cannot afford to just sit back and hope that the authorities will find them. They must become actively involved in the search themselves.

Children, however, aren't the only ones who turn up missing. Along with the nearly two million juveniles who run away from home annually, a large number of adults also disappear every year. As of January 1, 2008, the FBI's National Crime Information Center (NCIC) had 105,229 active missing person cases in its files. Of these, a little over 50,000 were adults.[14] But this is a very conservative number because for a missing adult to be in the FBI's file, the person reporting the event must show that:

1. The missing adult has a proven mental or physical disability.
2. The adult is missing after a catastrophe.
3. There is evidence that the disappearance was not voluntary.
4. There is a reasonable concern for the missing adult's safety.

Thus, these requirements exclude many adults who simply disappear but don't fit into any of the above categories. How many is that? No one really knows for sure because these cases, if reported, often remain in local police department files. The total is likely many times the number in the FBI's files. And while some of these adults disappear for very clear reasons, such as huge debts, decaying marriages, and so on, some people, as in the following incident, disappear for no apparent reason at all.

In December 2009, the very popular television program *America's Most Wanted* featured the case of David Cook of Amsterdam, Missouri. Unlike most of the individuals featured on this show, David wasn't wanted for a crime. Rather, David suddenly disappeared in 2008 without reason, and his family has not heard from him since. Family members are so concerned for David's safety that they have offered a $100,000 reward for information concerning his whereabouts.

The facts of the case are these: On November 19, 2008, David Cook reportedly told an employee of his that he had to meet someone that day, but didn't say who. However, when David didn't show up for a meeting with business partners later that day, and when he didn't show up for work that night, family members went to check on him. They found his red pickup truck parked at his house. They also found his wallet still in the house, but David was not at home. The only things missing from the house were David's cell phone, his glasses, and his money clip. The house, family members reported, showed no signs of a struggle.

David worked for the Kansas City Power and Light Company and also managed an 8,000-acre ranch. Because he had always been such a stable, responsible person, family members, though not knowing what had happened to him, couldn't believe that he would just leave. Instead, they feared the possibility that he might have fallen victim to foul play or that he had been injured somewhere on the ranch and needed help. However, a thorough search of the ranch, including the use of a bloodhound, didn't turn up any clues as to his whereabouts.

The family, in an attempt to locate David, eventually contacted Equusearch, a professional search and rescue group from Texas. This organization, along with using normal search procedures, also brought in unmanned drones to fly over the huge ranch in an attempt to find any clues as to David's disappearance. In addition, the searchers paid particular attention to the quarries in the area, using underwater cameras and sonar equipment. The group didn't find anything.

Because of the lack of results from the various searches, some family members now believe that David has been kidnapped and killed. Apparently, several years previous to his disappearance, David had testified in a federal fraud case and as a result of his testimony received several death threats. "There were some rough people around there," said David's sister, Judy Transue, of the fraud trial. "There was some conflict."[15]

Others believe that David's disappearance had something to do with 100 head of cattle that had been stolen from the ranch he managed. "Cattle theft is a way bigger problem than people realize," said Sergeant Greg Martin of the Missouri Highway Patrol.[16]

So what happened to David? Did he just decide that he wanted to start a new life somewhere else? Did he have an accident? Was there a kidnapping? A murder?

No one knows. But as I will show many times in this book, family members mustn't give up hope. Missing loved ones have often been located years after their disappearance, many times dead, but not always.

A good example of this is the Elizabeth Smart case. I and most other police officers had thought that Elizabeth Smart, the fourteen-year-old Utah girl who disappeared from her home in Salt Lake City in June 2002, was almost certainly dead. Yet she turned up alive nine months later. Even more recently, in August 2009, the police in Antioch, California, located Jaycee Lee Dugard, a twenty-nine-year-old woman who disappeared as a young girl and had been missing for eighteen years. As it turned out, she had been abducted and held captive all of this time. Naturally, family members and the police had thought her dead.

Of course, the problem with cases such as David Cook's is that when an adult suddenly and unexpectedly goes missing, family members don't know what to do other than call the police. However, the police often can't offer much help. Unlike runaways, there is no law against adults leaving home, so family members must be able to show clear evidence of foul play or imminent danger to the missing adult before the police will become actively involved. But in many cases of missing adults, families don't need outside help anyway. As I will show in the following anecdote, sometimes finding a missing person can be as easy as simply accessing a computer.

In November 2002, Edelmiro Navarro, a mentally-disabled man, wandered away from a group home in Tampa, Florida. He had been doing yard work at the home and suddenly went missing. At the time, his family, though concerned, didn't panic.

"He would wander off a lot, but he always came back," said his sister Shirley Hamstra.[17]

This time, however, Edelmiro didn't return and consequently his family contacted the authorities. They also had Edelmiro posted on several missing person websites. Yet, no clues as to his whereabouts arose. When several years passed, the family finally gave up hope of ever seeing him again.

"We thought he was dead," said his sister. "Every time they found a body in the river, we called the mortuary."[18]

But he wasn't dead. Several weeks after his disappearance, Edelmiro turned up at the Lakeland Regional Medical Center, about thirty-five miles northeast of Tampa. He carried the identification of a man from Pennsylvania, though no one knows how he obtained it. Although at first caretakers thought Edelmiro was the man on the identification he produced, an attempt to obtain veteran's benefits in that name quickly made them aware that the identification was not his. From then on, Edelmiro became known as simply John Doe. Because of his mental disability Edelmiro couldn't tell the medical personnel who he was or where he was from, and consequently the state of Florida placed him at the Valencia Hills Nursing Home.

He would remain there, known only as John Doe, until February 2006 when a nurse at the home began a computer search. During his time at the nursing home Edelmiro had occasionally mentioned landmarks that the staff recognized as being in Tampa. The nurse, therefore, began her computer search in the Tampa area. Within thirty minutes she found an old photograph of Edelmiro on a missing person website belonging to the North American Missing Persons Network (www.nampn.org). Soon afterward, the authorities reunited Edelmiro with his family.

"I couldn't believe it," his sister said. "I was crying."[19]

Although certainly not applicable to the above case, a point we will talk more about later in this book is that, before launching a search for a missing adult, thought must be given to the possibility that the person left because of problems he or she wanted to escape. While the David Cook and Edelmiro Navarro cases are obviously situations in which a search is justified, in many cases consideration must be given to the likelihood that a missing adult does not want to be found, but would rather be left alone to start a new life. The website for the North American Missing Persons Network tells of the case of a woman who disappeared, leaving food cooking on the stove and hungry cats in her home. Family members and friends naturally feared the worst, that she had been abducted. When finally located, though, the woman said that she simply needed a change in her life. Another good example of this situation happened several years ago in Kentucky.

In May 2005, the mother of Brandi Stahr was in the process of having her daughter, who had disappeared seven years earlier in Texas, declared legally dead. Brandi had been a sophomore at Texas A & M University in 1998 when, after an argument with her mother about poor grades, she disappeared. At the time though, the disagreement with her mother hadn't seemed that important, and the police handled the case as a crime. Fearing she had been abducted and murdered, the authorities searched a nearby woods and even questioned a serial rapist on Death Row about her disappearance. The years passed with no news of Brandi, and family members began to accept that she was likely dead.

However, in May 2005, Texas Rangers and U.S. Marshals, working on an anonymous tip, found Brandi alive and well in Florence, Kentucky, a suburb of Cincinnati. She had worked there as a department manager at the local Sam's Club for five years. She hadn't been abducted. She had simply disappeared on her own.

"I wouldn't say she was scared," said Chris Riley, a U.S. Marshal in Cincinnati. "But she knew what was going on."[20] It was apparent to those who located her that Brandi knew exactly what was occurring, and that she definitely wasn't happy about being found.

"She was trying to keep a low profile, which she successfully did," said Jack Hildebrand of the U.S. Marshal's Office in Columbus, Ohio. "She basically didn't do any of the normal things people do."[21]

What Marshal Hildebrand is talking about is that, although keeping and using her real name, Brandi did not obtain a Kentucky driver's license, nor did she have any utility bills put in her name, common ways to locate someone through a computer search. Interestingly enough, along with using her real name, Brandi also used her real social security number and paid taxes under it. Yet, because of privacy laws, law enforcement officers could not access Social Security Administration or Internal Revenue Service records.

"We thought we were dealing with a missing persons case," said Texas Ranger Frank Malinak. "But, in actuality, we were dealing with a person who did not want to be found and was in hiding."[22]

Once the story of Brandi's disappearance and recovery became known, many members of the news media naturally tried to contact her. Brandi, however, didn't want to talk to them. She did give the authorities a telephone number for her family to call, but said she wasn't ready yet for a visit.

Brandi's mother, however, wouldn't accept this. "We're going. I'm going," she said. "Even if I have to sit out in a (Sam's Club) parking lot to see her."[23]

Brandi's case, though interesting, is by no means unique. On the website for the North American Missing Persons Network, of the seventy-nine missing persons on their list who have been found, forty were alive. Many, like Brandi, really didn't want to be found, even though family members have often anguished for years over their disappearance.

Interestingly, Brandi's family, if they had known what to do, could have located her years earlier. And even though Brandi obviously didn't want to renew her relationship with them, at least family members would have known she was okay. "A licensed, bonded investigator can purchase information from various companies that buy aggregate data from the U.S. government and make it available for a fee," said Robert Townsend of the National Association of Legal Investigators, commenting on how he would have found Brandi.[24]

When I headed the Indianapolis Police Department's Homicide Branch we used one of these companies to find witnesses in murder cases who had disappeared. Quite often, murder cases can take a year or two, or even longer, before going to trial, and witnesses can many times disappear during this period. The company we used was extremely thorough and almost always came up with useful information about a person's present whereabouts. Later in this book, I will share with readers the names of some of these companies. With this search possibility available, families will then have to decide on their own whether or not the person really wants to be found. Many times, however, family members don't want to confront the person, but only be certain that he or she is alive and well. This method will give families that option.

On the other hand, family members and the authorities many times know with certainty that some individuals are not missing of their own volition, that they have not left because of the desire to start a new life, but rather are missing because they have been the victim of a crime. High-profile cases such as that of Natalee Holloway, the eighteen-year-old who disappeared while on a high school senior trip to Aruba, illustrate instances in which family members and the authorities feel absolutely certain the missing person has not dropped out of sight voluntarily, but rather has been the victim of foul play. Even these individuals will many times turn up, though most times deceased.

The FBI's NCIC network, for example, as of January 1, 2008, had 6,945 unidentified deceased individuals in its files, with an average of 1,400 new cases being added every year.[25] Even worse, over 40,000 sets of human remains, which have also not been identified, sit in coroners' and medical examiners' offices across the country, with thousands more turning up every year.[26] These are all people someone is missing. However, with the new DNA methods now available, which we will discuss later, positive identification can be made on recovered remains that family members believe may be those of a missing loved one.

Finally, as medical science continues to improve and people live longer and longer lives, a new problem has emerged: increasing numbers of elderly people with memory and cognitive disabilities. Because of these problems, elderly family members can often wander away from home, become confused, and eventually go missing.

How many elderly people become missing and endangered every year in our country? Again, as with other types of missing individuals, no one knows for sure. An article in the *Boston Globe* states that estimates put the number of Alzheimer's patients reported to the police as missing at around 32,000 annually.[27] The problem is so acute that more than two dozen states have begun issuing Silver Alerts. Similar to Amber Alerts, which are television announcements, electronic road sign messages, and cell phone alerts that make the public aware of missing children in danger; Silver Alerts make the public aware of the missing elderly who are in danger.

How dangerous is it for an elderly person to become missing? On October 5, 2005, seventy-seven-year-old Benton Abney disappeared. He was last seen leaving his home in Harvey, Illinois, a suburb of Chicago, driving a 2003 Nissan Sentra. Benton suffered from dementia and memory loss. When he didn't arrive at the location he said he was going to, family members reported his disappearance, and the police in Lake County, Indiana, located his car in a ditch the next day, but he wasn't in it. On February 22, 2006, a farmer in northwest Indiana found the badly decomposed body of Benton Abney. He had apparently wandered away after his car became stuck in the ditch.

The female elderly are just as much at risk. Stella Dickerman, the eighty-three-year-old mother of Marianne Dickerman Caldwell, wandered away from a high school softball game in Rindge, New Hampshire. Marianne naturally became frantic because her mother suffered from Alzheimer's. Three years later, several hunters came across Stella's remains in a nearby woods. "There's just something dreadful about being unfound and out in the woods," said Caldwell.[28]

Like young children who run away, the missing elderly can quickly fall victim to many hazards, and so finding them as soon as possible is imperative. And again, as with runaways, family members mustn't depend totally on the authorities to locate the missing elderly, but must take an active part themselves, using the methods I will outline.

In the next chapter we will begin our discussion on runaways. We will look at the reasons many children run away from home. With this information, concerned parents can lessen the likelihood that one of their own children will become a runaway.

Why Do Children Run Away?

$\mathcal{I}$n July 2009, Kortney Jones of Shepardsville, Kentucky, looked out the window of her home and saw two children, a boy and a girl, walking down the road carrying several bags. They appeared to her to be much too young to be out walking by themselves, and so she ran out and persuaded the young boy and girl to come into her house. Once inside, the boy, who turned out to be ten years old, told Ms. Jones that he and his six-year-old sister had run away from home because their mother's boyfriend had beaten them. After hearing the children's story, Ms. Jones decided she needed to contact the Bullitt County Sheriff's Department and let them handle this situation.

"They had marks on their backs, arms, and legs where they had been beaten with a belt, they stated," said Lieutenant Scott McGaha of the Bullitt County Sheriff's Department.[1]

The ten-year-old boy, a seemingly resourceful young man, had not only taken money with him when he and his sister ran away, but also pillows, toys, a screwdriver for protection, and a GPS device in the event they became lost. Upon hearing the children's story, the Sheriff's Department sent deputies to their home. There, they found the runaways' twenty-eight-year-old mother and her forty-three-year-old boyfriend intoxicated and passed out, apparently unaware that the children had left. The deputies also found a three-year-old in the house, unattended and covered with paint. Later investigation discovered that the runaway children had been beaten because they had apparently made too much noise while playing hide-and-go-seek. Deputies arrested the

mother and boyfriend, charging them both with Wanton Endanger-
ment, and the boyfriend also with Assault. The Sheriff's Department
then turned the children over to the custody of their grandmother.

"They just wanted to get away," said Chris Carlsen, the ten-year-
old's father. "I know the little girl, she's not my child, but I love her like
my own. She is terrified of this man. He is trouble."[2]

It doesn't require too much imagination to see the danger these
two small children were in during their attempt to run away from
home. Even though the ten-year-old boy seemed to be very mature
for his age, considering the items he thought to bring with them, the
two children nevertheless still put themselves in extreme danger from
the dozens of things that could go wrong, such as passing traffic (they
were only about a half mile from Interstate 65), unrestrained animals,
uncovered holes, and many other possible dangers, to say nothing of
making themselves easy targets for human predators.

The above incident demonstrates one of the major reasons children run away from home every year in our country: to escape abuse at
home. The ten- and six-year-old, living under the authority of a violent
adult, likely saw no alternative other than running away. Although I
don't know the intricacies of these children's home life, I have seen
many times over my career in law enforcement that physical abuse like
this seldom just stops on its own. Rather, unless acted upon by the
authorities, it usually increases in intensity over time.

Another interesting case of a child feeling forced to run away
from home, this one involving alleged threatened physical abuse, and
possibly even murder, occurred in Ohio in July 2009. Rifqa Bary, a
seventeen-year-old girl raised as a Muslim, converted to Christianity.
She ran away from home, according to news reports, because she feared
for her life due to her religious conversion.

Rifqa told reporters that her father "said he would kill me or send
me back to Sri Lanka," where she said he told her, "they have asylums
where they put people like me."[3]

Rifqa eventually ended up living with a Christian family in Florida, who fought an intense legal battle to keep her from being returned

to her home in Ohio. This case languished in various courts in Ohio and Florida until August 2010, when Rifqa turned eighteen and could no longer be forced to return home. Her parents, during the entire incident, vehemently denied any intent to cause her harm.

However, physical violence isn't the only type of abuse that children run away from home to escape. Many children also run away to escape sexual abuse in the home. This type of abuse, to both boys and girls, is much more prevalent in our country than the public would ever suspect. According to U.S. Department of Justice statistics, over two-thirds of the victims of sexual assault reported to the police are under the age of eighteen, 14 percent of them under the age of six. Further statistics show that the majority (77 percent) of sexual assaults against children take place within a home.[4] Also, an article in *USA Today* states that 70 to 90 percent of the sexual assaults against children are committed by people known to the children, and that 30 to 40 percent of them are committed by relatives.[5]

Often unfortunately, one or both parents may be unaware that a family member or someone close to the family is sexually abusing one or all of their children. The children, on the other hand, can often be too frightened or too ashamed to tell about it, or they may fear that they won't be believed if they do tell about it. These children many times find that the only recourse for them is to run away from the home where this sexual abuse is occurring.

"When I turned thirteen, my mom found a new partner who lived at home with us," a girl named Rebecca said when asked why she had run away. "He raped me regularly and abused my younger sisters as well."[6]

A word of advice to parents who are totally baffled and can't figure out why their child, who seems to be a really good kid, would want to run away from home: sexual abuse is a real possibility. Unlike physical abuse, sexual abuse seldom leaves any visible signs that would make parents aware it is occurring. However, sexual abuse of children occurs at an alarmingly large rate in our country. Studies show that one out of every six boys and one out of every four girls in the United States will be sexually assaulted before they reach their eighteenth birthday.[7]

Fortunately, while the physical signs may not be visible, there are many behavioral signs of sexual abuse, which concerned parents will find that I detail extensively in my book *Sex Crimes Investigation*.[8]

Consequently, parents baffled about the reason a child has run away from home should never believe that there is absolutely no way their child could have been sexually molested or believe that some person simply could not be a molester. Child molesters often disguise themselves as the least likely person. One thing I learned through my years in law enforcement is that absolutely anyone can be a child molester. One has only to think of the scandal in the Catholic Church and several other large institutions to realize how true this is.

Of course, it is also possible for sexual abuse that makes children want to run away to be perpetrated outside the home. The following is an example of a young girl who was the victim of just such an incident.

"I was 15 when I left home. There were many reasons that I am sure most kids go through, but when I had an experience with date rape and told my mother, who said 'it was my fault and what did I expect?' I decided to bolt. I figured I could take care of myself better than anyone so I left."[9]

Most children, when experiencing something traumatic like this, expect their parents to be there for them. Obviously, the young girl above didn't feel that her mother was, and so she left. Quite often, child welfare workers find, a lack of love and concern by parents will be the impetus for children to become runaways. These workers find that many times the parents of runaways are deeply involved in their careers; engrossed in trying to make their own romantic relationships work; deeply immersed into substance abuse, be it alcohol, prescription drugs, or illegal drugs; or involved in some other activity that keeps them from paying attention to their children.

"I started running away when I was 10 or 11," said a young girl named Amanda. "It all started when my mom started drinking again. I couldn't take it anymore; she just kept leaving me with my brothers and sister. How, I kept asking myself, would I take care of them, when I was just a kid myself?"[10]

Amanda ran away from home, but returned when her mother promised to straighten up, stop drinking, and let her be a child again.

The promise didn't last long though. Amanda's mother almost immediately began drinking again and soon left the children alone for three days. After dropping her siblings off at a store, Amanda ran away once more, but this time she moved in with three men in their twenties, all of whom had sex with her as payment for her staying there.

A thirteen-year-old runaway tells another story of not getting the love or attention a child needs. "The feeling of being lonely and unwanted came when I was 13. My mom had been with her boyfriend for a couple of years and I felt that he got the attention I was supposed to be receiving, so I started looking for love and acceptance outside of home. . . . The second day before my 14th birthday I decided to run away."[11]

Another thirteen-year-old runaway, when asked why she left home, told a counselor, "I just don't feel like I'm taken care of like a daughter should be."[12]

Citing similar feelings, a young runaway said, "My parents don't like me. I get good grades but I'm not popular. I babysit for pay, but my mom keeps all my money. I only have a few friends, but my mother hates them."[13]

In a further case, a fourteen-year-old runaway's mother abused drugs as well as alcohol, but a lack of love and attention wasn't the only reason that the child ran away. Along with the mother ignoring her children, her substance abuse habit became so intense that it drained the family resources, and there was not enough money to feed them all. "I would rather run away than have my sister go hungry," said the fourteen-year-old.[14]

Along with a lack of love and attention, another reason for becoming a runaway, especially among teenagers, is that many youths feel a strong urge to be independent, and consequently chaff at the restrictions and rules imposed in their home. Many of these children long to be free of parental oversight and control, to be able to do whatever they want, with whomever they want. They want a life with no curfew, no chores, no homework. Just fun. For example, in 2008, the police in a large city received a call to take the report of a teenage boy who ran away from home because his father wouldn't let him play video games until he had finished his homework.

The following teenage runaway also chaffed under the rules in her home. "I didn't like it there [home] because it was so strict and [there were] so many rules, and I wanted to do what I wanted to do," said a sixteen-year-old runaway. "I felt like I was so closed in that I didn't have any freedom at all."[15]

While the two children above may sound spoiled and selfish, their motives for running away are not that uncommon. According to the National Runaway Switchboard, a parent being too strict is a very common reason they hear for why a child ran away. The National Runaway Switchboard is a Chicago-based organization that offers runaway children both counseling and help in finding needed resources, such as food and shelter. It is in addition a location at which a runaway can leave a message for his or her family, and also check for a message from his or her family.

The rules and restrictions teenagers hate most, however, often involve dating. "I was dating a guy that my parents hated right from the start," said a fifteen-year-old runaway. "Through the week I wasn't allowed out at all. Weekends came with a curfew of 9:00 P.M. This was so unfair. When was I to spend time with who I was sure would be my husband?"[16] Eventually, in response to the restrictions set by her parents, the girl ran away from home with her boyfriend.

Sometimes, drastic changes in a family structure will cause youngsters to feel that their new lives are intolerable and that running away is the only option. When parents die, divorce, separate, or when parents begin dating or get remarried, often bringing new stepchildren into the family, youngsters can feel left out, can feel not loved any longer. Or, just as bad, they can find themselves having to share the love and attention, along with the family resources, that before had been all theirs. These children can many times feel that the changes in their lives are intolerable and believe that running away will make things better. Unfortunately, the parents in their new romantic relationship, or parents starting their lives over without a relationship, are often so consumed with how the changes affect them that they don't see how their children are affected.

I can certainly relate to how these children feel. My mother died when I was twelve, leaving my father with five children. He eventually met a woman who was divorced with six children, and they married. Suddenly, our house became very small, and getting into the bathroom became a quest. What was once a family of four boys and one girl exploded into a family of eight boys and three girls. Suddenly, resources like hot water and snack food became rare. Also, I found myself having to share my home with strangers that I had nothing in common with. In addition, a new person I didn't know, and who at the time I certainly didn't think of as my mother, suddenly began issuing rules and discipline. Did I think about running away? Sure I did.

Fortunately, I soon discovered that having a large family has advantages. Home life was never boring, since there always seemed to be something going on. In addition, my stepmother turned out to be a wonderful woman who gave love and attention equally to all the children. But really important, I attended a tough inner-city high school. However, since I hung out with my brothers and stepbrothers we were numerous enough to never have any trouble with the toughs and bullies.

How common is this reason for running away from home? A 2007 report from the National Runaway Switchboard showed that changing family dynamics, such as divorce, arrival of stepparents, and new sibling rivalry, accounted for nearly 30 percent of their calls in 2006.[17]

Also, quite often children, having had limited life experiences, see life in general as being unfair. So, when things don't go well, running away becomes the answer for them. For example, a woman's twelve-year-old diabetic daughter ran away from home, leaving her insulin behind. The daughter's reason for running away? She was tired of it and didn't want to be a diabetic any longer. Interestingly, a study from the University of Iowa found that children with disabilities such as this have twice the likelihood of running away as children without disabilities.[18]

In addition to all of the above reasons for children running away from home, there are many others, including: having a fight with their parents, because the parents themselves fight constantly, because of a change in home location, to escape punishment for some misdeed, to avoid some future experience that the children feel certain will be unpleasant or embarrassing, because the children are heavily hooked on drugs and don't want their parents to find out, or because the children fear the consequences of telling their parents that they are pregnant or have gotten someone pregnant. Along with this, gay children will often run away from home because they fear their parents' or friends' reactions when these individuals find out about their sexual orientation. Finally, children will occasionally run away from home as a bargaining ploy to force their parents to give in on some point they disagree on.

While much of the information I have given so far in this chapter is anecdotal, a number of scientific studies have also investigated why children run away. For example, a study conducted at Iowa State University interviewed over 300 runaways and many of their parents, along with an equal number of families without a runaway problem. The study came up with some not totally unexpected findings. As might be imagined, there was much more dysfunction in the families of runaways as opposed to families without runaways, and also much less warmth and acceptance. Over half of the runaways said that they felt neglected, a third of the female runaways reported sexual abuse, and two-thirds of all the runaways reported physical abuse.[19]

A further study, this one conducted by the U.S. Department of Health and Human Services, found that 46 percent of runaways reported being physically abused. Another 17 percent reported being sexually abused, and 38 percent emotionally abused.[20]

Lastly, some children run away from home not because of abuse, family structure changes, strict rules, or any of the other reasons above. They do it simply because they are bored and want some excitement.

"When I was 17 years old, I ran away from home, determined never to go back," said a runaway. "I wasn't a bad kid, actually if you ask my parents I was the perfect kid. I didn't get into trouble. I followed the rules. I got good grades, didn't party. To other kids my age I was boring."[21]

Another young person expressed much of the same sentiment. "I am 17 years old. I don't know why I want to run away from home. My parents aren't bad people, they don't abuse me, and everyone around me is happy. But still I hate it all. I hate the monotony of it all. I hate how everything is so predictable."[22]

Readers can see from what we've discussed so far that there are many reasons why children run away from home, some of which should be very apparent to the parents, some not quite so apparent, and some likely invisible even to the best of parents. Often, when children are experiencing what they see as unbearable stress in their lives, running away seems to be the only solution. Sometimes this stress is the parent's fault, but sometimes it's not.

And as we have also seen in this chapter, many times children can run away from home for reasons having nothing to do with intense stress, family dysfunction, poor parenting, or abuse. Sometimes the children of even good parents simply want to experience new things and to test boundaries. And so, even in families where the parents have done an excellent job of raising the children, there can be a runaway.

Yet, while almost two million children a year in our country run away from home, many times to the complete surprise of their parents, who see themselves as, and often actually are, good parents, another possibility must be considered before labeling a child who has not returned home as a runaway. This is especially true for children who have never displayed any behavioral problems that would indicate that they could become a runaway. As we will talk about in the next chapter, parents must also consider the possibility that their children, rather than running away, have been abducted. Child abduction occurs much more often in our country than most readers would suppose and, as we will discuss in the next chapter, finding these abducted children quickly can be paramount to saving their lives.

• 3 •

Runaway or Abduction?

$\mathscr{F}$ ifteen-year-old Tracy Gilpin left a party in Kingston, Massachusetts, to make a quick stop at a nearby Cumberland Farms convenience store. But she never returned. Her family, naturally alarmed, reported her disappearance to the police. The authorities, however, didn't think the situation was all that serious and listed her as simply a runaway.

"The police deemed her a runaway and wrote her off," said Tracy's mother Kathleen Gilpin. "They came to me several times and said she had been seen at the beach or the mall."[1]

Three weeks after Tracy's disappearance, a woman walking her dog in a state park in nearby Plymouth, Massachusetts, stumbled onto Tracy's body. Someone had crushed her skull. Despite the police reports of her being seen several times, an autopsy showed that Tracy had died soon after her disappearance.

In a similar case, witnesses last saw thirteen-year-old Mayra Cruz at a school bus stop in Hartford, Connecticut. They told the police that they saw her there in a small yellow car driven by a young man. Although her family reported her as missing, the authorities initially believed that she had left home willingly and classified her as a runaway. The police even later stated that they had at least three witnesses who had seen Mayra around the Hartford area.

A month after her family reported Mayra as missing, her body turned up in a wooded area in East Windsor, Connecticut, about ten miles northeast of Hartford. The police theorized she had been murdered and then dumped there. She still wore the same clothing she'd had on the day she disappeared.

In December 2008, the police arrested Pedro Miranda and charged him with the murder of Mayra and two other females. The police now believe that Miranda, a registered sex offender, had apparently abducted Mayra before killing her. They charged him not only with murder but also with kidnapping.

In another case, this one in July 1974, thirteen-year-old Lisa White disappeared from Vernon, Connecticut. She had gone that day to visit a nearby friend, but vanished on the trip home. The police immediately classified her as a runaway, saying that she had been seen afterward at a nearby mall. Her mother, however, insisted that Lisa was not a runaway but instead had been abducted.

"They didn't give two hoots when my daughter disappeared," said Lisa's mother, Kelly. "A mother knows when something bad happens to their child, and I knew deep down Lisa was never coming home."[2]

The local police department now also believes that Lisa was likely abducted. Her mother has kept the same telephone number since 1974 in the hope that her daughter might eventually call.

What the three incidents above have in common is that in each case the police department originally assumed that a missing youngster had disappeared voluntarily, that the child was a runaway. While the police will be right in assuming this in the very large majority of cases in which a young person disappears without any evidence of foul play, this can nevertheless be an extremely dangerous assumption for the police to make and for the family to accept. While there are nearly two million runaways every year in the United States, there are also hundreds of thousands of child abductions. This crime can and does occur regularly in our country. How regularly?

The most extensive study of child abduction, which was published by the U.S. Department of Justice, is titled the *National Incidence Studies of Missing, Abducted, Runaway, and Thrownaway Children*. The researchers for this study gathered statistics from police departments all across the United States. In their report, they estimated that in 1999 there were 262,100 child abductions in the United States, 203,900 by family members and 58,200 by someone outside the family.[3] When I researched the figures through 2010, I found no reason to believe that these numbers have decreased at all. As a matter of fact, more recent studies have now put the annual number of child abductions in our country at nearly 350,000.[4]

Researchers into child abduction have found a number of motives for this crime. The most common reason is that the parent on the losing side of a child custody battle decides to take action in defiance of the court's decision. This parent either doesn't return a child after a visitation or simply abducts the child as he or she is leaving school, is in front of his or her home, or at some other location.

While in most parental child abductions the custodial parent knows exactly what has happened to the child, in those parental abductions in which the noncustodial parent takes the child at some time other than at the end of a visitation, custodial parents and the police may wrongly assume that the child, rather than being abducted, has simply run away from home. And while many readers might assume that a child abducted by a noncustodial parent is not in any danger, that certainly isn't the case. The following incident demonstrates just how dangerous a parental abduction can be.

In February 2007, forty-seven-year-old Eric Johnson had taken his eight-year-old daughter Emily on a week-long vacation to Cancun, Mexico. The agreement he'd had with his ex-wife, Beth, was that at the end of the visitation he would drop Emily off at her school in Bedford, Indiana, and then Beth would pick Emily up after school.

However, rather than taking Emily to school, Eric instead drove her to the Bedford City Airport. There, he rented a single-engine Cessna and flew off in it with her.

Eric and Beth's marriage had been filled with anger and fighting, and their divorce had been no different. Beth had even been forced to take out a protective order against Eric after he pulled a gun on her and threatened to kill her if she didn't stop the divorce proceedings.

On this day, when Beth checked to be certain that Eric had dropped Emily off at school and found that he hadn't, she immediately reported the abduction to the police. She also called her ex-husband on his cell phone. He reportedly told her, "I've got (Emily) and you're not going to get her back." Beth then heard Emily in the background crying, "Mommy, come get me!"[5]

Moments later, Eric crashed the Cessna into his ex-mother-in-law's house, killing both him and Emily. The mother-in-law, though home, wasn't injured.

In the above case, there was no question that Emily wasn't a runaway. However, parental abduction cases aren't always this clear cut. Therefore, the custodial parents of children who don't seem to have any behavioral problems and have disappeared must not just accept the verdict of the police that they are runaways. Instead, these parents must look into the possibility of a parental abduction. This can usually be very easy to verify because the abducting parent will most often disappear at the same time as the child.

There are a number of precautions that custodial parents who fear a parental abduction can take in order to prevent an abduction or to assure the quick return of their child if an abduction does occur. I go into great detail about these in my book *Child Abduction: Prevention, Investigation, and Recovery.*[6]

Occasionally also, a child is abducted by a family member other than a parent. There are various possible motives for this kind of abduction, but often the reason has to do with the family member worrying about the safety or welfare of the child. However, other much less benign reasons are also possible, including sexual assault.

Also occurring quite often, although less frequently than family abductions, are child abductions by an acquaintance. These abductions can occur for a number of reasons. Sometimes the child can be abducted by an acquaintance because the parents of the child are so bad that the person is worried about the welfare of the child. But more often the child is abducted by an acquaintance for the purpose of sexual assault, which, according to one report, is the case for 23 percent of all female acquaintance abductions.[7] For male victims, the motives behind acquaintance abduction are often robbery, physical assault, or gang retaliation. However, an important point for readers to remember is that, like the three victims at the beginning of this chapter, these young abduction victims are often assumed by the police to be simply runaways.

Not occurring nearly as often as the other types of child abduction, but almost always exceedingly more dangerous, are abductions of children by strangers. There are a number of reasons for these abductions, but the most common reason, especially in the abduction of girls, is sexual assault.

"Girls were the predominant victims of nonfamily abductions overall and of stereotypical kidnappings as well (65 percent and 69 percent, respectively), reflecting the frequency of sexual assault as a motive for many nonfamily abductions," said the "Nonfamily Abducted Children: National Estimates and Characteristics" section of the *National Incidence Studies of Missing, Abducted, Runaway, and Thrownaway Children*. The report then goes on to say, "Criminal assaults were a motive in most of the nonfamily abductions. Close to half of all nonfamily abduction victims and stereotypical kidnapping victims [58,200 in the study year] were sexually assaulted."[8]

With the advent of the Internet and all of its social networking sites, child sexual predators, who used to have to physically go out to parks, shopping centers, and other locations in order to find their abduction victims, no longer have to leave the comfort of their homes in order to find thousands and thousands of possible targets. All sexual predators need now is a computer with Internet access. Child sexual predators today typically go into Internet chat rooms, pretend to be an age-appropriate youngster, establish contact with underage targets, and then persuade the children to meet them.

An example of this occurred recently in Hamilton County, Indiana. Twenty-nine-year-old Samuel Henzel of Oak Park, Illinois, apparently made contact over the Internet with a twelve-year-old girl and arranged a meeting with her. The young girl rode her bicycle to a Westfield, Indiana, Comfort Suites motel, where authorities say Henzel sexually assaulted her. Henzel, after being arrested, reportedly told the police that he knew how old the girl was.[9] While it is uncertain whether this young girl knew the truth or not about whom she was meeting, in most cases like this, since the predators are not at all who they pretended to be on the Internet, the children can balk, and the meeting quickly become an abduction for the purpose of sexual assault.

Unfortunately, a large number of these abductors are child predators known to the police and often on the state's sex offender registry. Consequently, these individuals realize that if they are caught they face decades in prison. For this reason, they will often murder their victims after the sexual assault. Several studies have shown that if an abduction victim is to be murdered, this will likely happen within twenty-four hours of the abduction.

The Washington State Attorney General's Office conducted a study in which researchers looked at 775 child abductions that ended in murder. They found that in 76 percent of these cases, the child had been murdered within three hours of being abducted, and in 88.5 percent of the cases within twenty-four hours, usually after being sexually assaulted.[10] It is for this reason that parents who believe there is any chance at all that their children have been abducted must insist that the police treat the case as an abduction and not simply label it as a runaway case. As shown above, their children's lives can very well depend on this.

The major point I've tried to make in this chapter is that if parents believe their children, rather than running away, may have been abducted, then finding them quickly is essential to their safety. However, as we will see in the next chapter, finding runaway children quickly is also essential to their safety because many, many dangers face them when they are alone on the street.

· 4 ·

The Danger to Runaways

$\mathscr{T}$he Super Bowl is a huge economic boon for any city that hosts it. Thousands of people travel to the host city and spend millions of dollars enjoying the many cultural and entertainment activities the city has to offer. Unfortunately, the Super Bowl also draws individuals who cater to more unsavory tastes, and to the people who supply what these individuals are seeking. Just such an individual showed up in Miami in February 2010 for Super Bowl XLIV.

On Super Bowl weekend, the FBI in Miami arrested Fred Collins of Hawaii and charged him with Transporting and Causing a Minor to Engage in Commercial Sex Acts. According to a Department of Justice press release, Collins had brought two adult women and a juvenile female from Hawaii to Florida to engage in prostitution over the Super Bowl weekend. "Collins allegedly booked the victim's [juvenile female] travel under a false name," said the release, "paid for the victim's airfare and hotel lodging, and supervised and directed the victim's prostitution activities."[1] If convicted, Collins faces from ten years to life in prison.

"The Super Bowl is a big destination for child prostitution and adult prostitution," said Tom Simon, FBI Special Agent.[2]

How does this incident apply to the subject of this book? The victim in this case was a sixteen-year-old runaway girl Collins had met in Hawaii. Through various persuasive techniques, he convinced her to join his group of prostitutes.

"We're not only FBI agents, we're human beings, and these cases just break our hearts," said Agent Simon.[3]

This incident provides a clear example of what can happen to runaway children. Once away from home and its support system, runaway children will soon run out of money and resources. These children, facing the prospect of no sanitation facilities, no food, and no longer being able to sleep indoors, are then often forced to eat out of trash cans and sleep on the street or in parks. They are also forced to steal, beg, or find some way, which we will talk about below, to get the money necessary for basic survival.

"I made it all the way to North Carolina," said a thirteen-year-old runaway girl, "sleeping in the woods, bathing in gas station restrooms, and eating out of the trash."[4]

Another runaway, this one a fourteen-year-old boy named Larry, said on a runaway website, "I went through people's trash for food and slept anywhere I thought it was somewhat safe."[5]

A fifteen-year-old runaway from Huntington, West Virginia, named Steven White, tells of checking on the cleaning schedule for the restrooms at the local Wal-Mart. He knew that once the cleaning people had left it was safe to sleep in there.

Unfortunately, along with the prospect of going hungry and dirty, there are also many predators like Mr. Collins just waiting for these children. Readers will recall the quote in chapter 1 from the pimp of a runaway girl: "With young girls, you promise them heaven, they'll follow you to hell." As this man states, predators of young runaways will usually start off with a smooth, amicable tone, seeming to be a friend. These predators will then entice young runaway girls and boys to come and stay with them, using offers of food, clothing, shelter, and often drugs. But the runaway soon finds that he or she must do something in return, and that is to become a prostitute. Youths who refuse are often threatened or physically assaulted until they do agree. And unfortunately, the appetite of adults for young prostitutes is enormous. As the following incident illustrates, even football legend Lawrence Taylor got himself caught up in this.

On May 6, 2010, the police arrested NFL great Lawrence Taylor and charged him with Third-Degree Rape and Soliciting Prostitution. Allegedly, a friend arranged to have a prostitute brought to Lawrence

Taylor's room at the Holiday Inn in Rockland County, New York, about twenty-five miles north of New York City. Taylor, according to news reports, agreed to pay $300 for the girl's services.

The problem?

The girl was a sixteen-year-old runaway from the Bronx in New York City.

Following his arrest, Taylor bonded out of jail on $75,000 bail. In June 2010, a grand jury returned an indictment against Taylor, charging him with Rape in the Third Degree, Criminal Sexual Act in the Third Degree, Endangering the Welfare of a Child, Patronizing a Prostitute, and two counts of Sexual Abuse in the Third Degree. Although given the opportunity, Taylor declined to testify before the grand jury. At a court appearance in October 2010, Taylor's attorney said that a plea bargain remained a possibility.

"We have a victim who is 16 years old who has alleged that they had sex," said Christopher P. St. Lawrence, the town supervisor of Ramapo, New York. "She is not allowed under New York laws to have consensual sex."[6]

The runaway, reported missing from her home in March 2010, told the police that she had been staying with a thirty-six-year-old parolee named Rasheed Davis. They had apparently met at a bus stop.

"He chats her up," said New York City Police Department spokesperson Paul Browne. "She explains she doesn't have a place to stay. He provides one."[7] Unfortunately, the cost to the runaway for this place to stay was becoming a prostitute.

After the encounter with Lawrence Taylor, the sixteen-year-old, according to news reports, wanted out of the business. She texted her uncle and told him what had happened and where she and Rasheed were headed. She told her uncle that she hadn't wanted to go to Taylor's room, but that Rasheed had beaten her until she agreed to. The uncle contacted the police, who found the runaway girl and eventually arrested Taylor. The police also arrested Rasheed and charged him with Unlawful Imprisonment, Assault, and Endangering the Welfare of a Child.

In January 2011, Taylor entered into a plea agreement. He pled guilty to two misdemeanor charges involving his sexual interaction with the runaway girl. A judge sentenced him to six years of probation and also required him to register as a sex offender. The young victim told the news media that she thought Taylor should have been sent to jail.

A 2009 article in the *New York Times* stated that a variety of studies have revealed that one-third of runaways will engage in trading sex for food, drugs, or a place to stay. But, the article warned, this bartering system can, and often does, quickly escalate into more formalized prostitution.[8] According to figures from the U.S. Department of Health and Human Services, there are as many as 300,000 child prostitutes in the United States, many of them runaways.[9] A study completed by the University of Pennsylvania found that 55 percent of young girls living on the street engage in formal prostitution, and that the average age that these girls begin is twelve to fourteen, while for boys it is eleven to thirteen.[10] A study reported in the *Journal of Sex Research* found that 13 percent of homeless and runaway boys reported exchanging sex for money or drugs.[11] Since these encounters usually involve having sex with older men, the risk of HIV to these young runaway boys is great.

Because of all the many thousands of runaway children, both boys and girls, forced into prostitution, the FBI in 2003 formed the Innocence Lost program. This is a group of agents who target the organizers of child prostitution. As of November 2010, the agents working for the Innocence Lost program had rescued more than 1,200 children from organized prostitution and had won convictions against more than 600 pimps, madams, and others involved in the commercial sex trade.[12] And while the efforts of this group are certainly commendable, readers should keep in mind that this is only a very tiny percentage of the number of children involved in prostitution, many of them runaways.

"It's definitely worsening," said Sergeant Kelley O'Connell of the Boston Police Department. "Gangs used to sell drugs. Now many of them have shifted to selling girls because it's just as lucrative but far less risky."[13]

Of course, being forced into prostitution isn't the only danger facing runaways. Many of these youngsters can also be forced to take part in pornographic productions. Like the market for young prostitutes, the market for child pornography is huge and, as the first incident below demonstrates, can involve individuals few would expect to be involved.

In January 2004, a thirteen-year-old runaway told the police that she had posed for pornography in an apartment in Mount Vernon, Illinois. When the police raided the apartment they found an enormous collection of child pornography: more than 1,000 CDs and seven computers filled with photos and videos of children engaging in sex. The police eventually arrested six men who they said were involved in this operation, including Jarrod Griffith, a junior high basketball coach, and David T. Cameron, a teacher at the Brehm Preparatory Academy in Carbondale, Illinois.

"It was disgusting," said Mount Vernon Police Chief Chris Mendenall. "They manufactured this not only for their own gratification, but to profit from it."[14]

David T. Cameron, following his conviction, stood in court on April 17, 2009, waiting for his judgment. The court sentenced him to ten years in prison for his part in the child pornography ring.

In another case, in June 2010, the police in Hagerstown, Maryland, arrested thirty-nine-year-old Michael William Zimmer and forty-three-year-old Robert William Mulkern and charged them with multiple criminal counts stemming from the production of child pornography that featured a fifteen-year-old runaway. The runaway's mother had contacted the police and told them that she thought her daughter might be in the company of Mulkern.

Although the incidents we've discussed so far are certainly disturbing, many readers may wonder just how prevalent is the sex trade, including both prostitution and child pornography, among runaways? A professor at the University of Toledo conducted a study which found that one out of every three runaways in Ohio gone for more than two weeks became involved in the sex trade. The report showed that, in 2009, Ohio had 3,056 runaways who had been missing from home for longer than two weeks. Thirty-five percent of them, or 1,070 runaways, became involved in the sex trade.

"These are disturbing facts," said Ohio Attorney General Richard Cordray about this study. "According to the report, it is estimated that in Ohio more than a thousand young people between the ages of twelve and seventeen have been trafficked into the sex trade over the course of a year."[15]

Young runaways, in addition to prostitution and pornography, also face the danger of falling into the company of individuals who use illegal drugs, either by running away with them or by encountering them after running away. Because of their close proximity to these individuals, runaways, who no longer have parents or other adults to intervene, can be tempted to try the drugs. Also, runaways may be enticed into trying illegal drugs by someone who wants to hook them into becoming a constant customer. An article about the dangers to runaways, which appeared on *OregonLive.com*, said, "If we don't get good guys out there to save them, believe me, the bad guys—the pimps, the drug dealers—will reach them. To the bad guys, kids are simply meat, are simply stooges for their criminal efforts."[16]

Again, like the sex trade, readers may wonder just how prevalent the use of illegal drugs is among runaways. Probably much worse than most readers would suspect. In three National Institute on Drug Abuse studies, researchers found that runaway youth had a markedly higher rate of illegal drug use than children who lived at home, and that runaways were also more likely to use more dangerous drugs. One of the studies found that three-fourths of the street youth questioned were using marijuana, one-third were using hallucinogens, and a fourth were using crack or some other form of cocaine.

"These very high rates of drug abuse underscore the critical need for intervention and treatment services for runaway and homeless youth, a need that is not being adequately met," said one of the researchers conducting the studies, Dr. Christopher Ringwalt of the Research Triangle Institute in Research Triangle Park, North Carolina.[17]

In another study, this one reported in the journal *Addictive Behaviors*, researchers interviewed over 300 runaways. They found that 71 percent of the runaways reported alcohol use and 46 percent reported drug use, with over a fourth stating that they had used alcohol or drugs at least once a week during the previous three months. The researchers also found symptoms of substance abuse in 47 percent of the runaways, while 17 percent of those studied reported being addicted to drugs.[18]

But of course, it isn't only drug pushers who will entice runaway children to try dangerous substances. As the following incident demonstrates, it can also be our neighbors.

On March 10, 2007, police officers went to a home in Bloomfield, Colorado, searching for a fifteen-year-old runaway boy, whose parents thought he might be staying there with a sixteen-year-old girl. At the home, the police did indeed find the runaway boy, but they also found something else. They discovered that the fifteen-year-old had been drinking vodka, allegedly supplied by the sixteen-year-old girl's mother, thirty-nine-year-old Amie Lynn Kresha. The boy's blood alcohol content measured .111, which is above the level considered to be intoxicated. The fifteen-year-old runaway, however, wasn't the only child not related to Kresha found in the house, and he wasn't the only child there drinking liquor.

"We found seven juveniles ranging from age ten to seventeen inside the house, and we had reason to believe at least two of them had been drinking," said Sergeant Colleen O'Connell of the Bloomfield Police Department.[19] The children told the police that they had been partying at Kresha's the previous evening.

A little over two weeks later, the police returned to Kresha's house, this time searching for a sixteen-year-old runaway girl. They found her, but again also found several other runaway teenagers in the house, several of whom had been drinking alcohol allegedly supplied by Kresha.

The mother of the sixteen-year-old runaway girl told the local newspaper, "This thing is way out of control. Apparently, she befriends all of these kids because she wants to be the cool party mom."[20]

In April of 2007, a court sentenced Kresha to a year in the county jail, but interestingly enough not for the alcohol charges, which hadn't yet come to trial. A court instead convicted her for an incident that occurred in February 2007, in which she allegedly took a fifteen-year-old girl not related to her to a tattoo parlor, where she claimed she was the girl's mother so that the fifteen-year-old could get a tattoo.

A runaway's life is one filled with temptations that can lead to danger. A study of runaway youth in San Francisco, Denver, and New York City found that 98 percent of the runaways questioned reported having consensual sexual intercourse, the majority without the use of a condom, which of course greatly increases the threat of HIV and other sexually transmitted diseases. Another 97 percent of those questioned reported using alcohol or drugs, with 21 percent admitting using injected drugs, which greatly increases the chances of infectious disease.[21]

And as if what we've talked about so far isn't enough to give parents nightmares, in addition to all the dangers we've discussed, runaways also face the threat of malnutrition, childhood diseases (runaways are very unlikely to get their vaccinations), frostbite, robbery, and physical assault. Runaways with health problems such as asthma or diabetes, of course, greatly increase their chances of having a serious or fatal episode. Along with all of this, young runaway girls are also particularly vulnerable to sexual assault. A study completed by the Iowa Department of Human Rights found that 12 percent of runaway girls, as the following incidents illustrate, reported being sexually assaulted.[22]

On April 9, 2010, in Victorville, California, a fifteen-year-old girl, who had run away from home because she had gotten into trouble at school, managed to make a frantic telephone call, pleading for help and saying that she had been sexually assaulted by two men who were still nearby. The men had picked up the runaway at a liquor store and persuaded her to accompany them to a nearby apartment. The police arrived and arrested the two men, charging them with Lewd Acts with a Child.

The police in Austin, Texas, on September 29, 2010, arrested two men and charged them with Attempted Aggravated Sexual Assault. Reportedly, one of the men gave beer to a thirteen-year-old runaway girl, who drank so much that she passed out. When she awoke, the two men were holding her down and attempting to have sex with her. She began screaming, and the men let her go and fled.

In November 2010, the Lincoln, Nebraska, police arrested a nineteen-year-old man and charged him with Sexual Assault of a Child. The incident involved a fourteen-year-old runaway girl.

As we talked about in chapter 1, almost two million children in our country run away from home every year. Many of these children are found by their parents or the police, while many others return home on their own. But a percentage of runaways, estimated at around 5 percent, or about 100,000 each year, aren't found or don't return home on their own. What happens to them?

Some of these runaways simply survive until they reach the age of majority and then go on with their lives. But others are not so lucky. According to a publication from Penn State University, approximately 5,000 runaway and homeless youth die each year from assault, illness, and suicide.[23] Also, a number of runaways, as the following incidents illustrate, don't survive their time on the street because of the predators they are forced to deal with.

According to the *LA Weekly News*, "Raven [real name: Alyssa Gomez] was one of the youngest and toughest Hollywood street runaways, living in alleys and back lots where beatings, drugs, and prostitution are still common. Addicted to meth, the stunningly beautiful fifteen-year-old foster kid and runaway turned tricks to buy drugs."[24]

However, on June 4, 2007, a thirty-eight-year-old man named Gilton Pitre, a convicted rapist and drug dealer, who had been released from prison just four days earlier, murdered Raven. He strangled her to death in an alley behind a restaurant on Sunset Boulevard in Los Angeles. Why he did it no one is sure.

"Something is terribly wrong when one of our kids can slip through the cracks and end up in an alleyway," said Los Angeles County Deputy District Attorney Sam Hulefeld.[25]

A jury, on May 3, 2010, convicted Pitre of Raven's murder. A judge sentenced him to 110 year in prison.

In a similar story, on July 30, 2010, a judge in Riverside, California, levied the death penalty against twenty-two-year-old Roman Gabriel Aldana, a man convicted in the murder of a sixteen-year-old runaway girl named Kayla Wood. Reportedly, Kayla met her murderer on the street and he persuaded her to accompany him to a friend's home. There, Kayla lived for a time with three men, using sex to pay for her rent. On the morning of the murder, one of the men slashed Kayla's throat with a razor, then one of the others stabbed her 133 times. Following this, the three men allegedly submerged Kayla's body in a bathtub full of water to be certain she was dead. They then set the home on fire in an attempt to cover up the crime.

"As the victim was terrified and begged him to stop, the defendant heartlessly ignored her cries for help," said Riverside County Superior Court Judge Jean P. Leonard upon Aldana's sentencing. "His actions were cold, callous, and brutal."[26]

A jury also found eighteen-year-old Jose Alfredo Solorza guilty of First-Degree Murder, Torture, and Arson. He received a sentence of thirty-one years in prison. Nineteen-year-old Anthony Bobadilla agreed to testify against the other two and pleaded guilty to Voluntary Manslaughter, Kidnapping, Arson, and Sexual Penetration with a Foreign Object. He received a sentence of twenty-three years in prison.

"I am extremely happy we are finally able to get Kayla the justice she deserves in death that she wasn't able to get in life," said Deputy District Attorney John Henry.[27]

The reason for Kayla's murder? The men thought the runaway girl might be pregnant.

Finally, a fate for some of the runaways who never return home is suicide, a much bigger risk among runaways than most people would suspect. The studies discussed earlier from the National Institute on Drug Abuse found that nearly a third of the street youth they interviewed had tried to kill themselves at least once. The rate was even higher for those youths who had a serious drug abuse problem.[28]

As can be seen by the incidents in this chapter, the world for runaway children can be an exceedingly dangerous place. This is why the parents of runaways cannot and should not depend totally on the police to find their children. There are simply too many runaways reported to the police every year for them to mount any type of serious search. And this is also why it is so critically important for parents to get involved in the search for their runaway children. Their children's welfare and very lives can depend on being found as quickly as possible. By following the advice I give in the next chapter, parents can greatly increase the chances of finding their runaway children before some tragedy can befall them.

• 5 •

Finding Runaways

𝒯ollowing a fight with her parents, Jamie Stevens, a fifteen-year-old girl living in Redmond, Washington, a suburb of Seattle, bolted out the door and ran away from home. Eight days later, on September 29, 2009, Jamie sent her mother an e-mail saying that she was sorry and would be home soon. However, the next day Jamie updated her MySpace account with a message saying that she didn't know what to do. Jamie's parents then received some information from several of Jamie's MySpace friends saying that they believed she might have joined up with a couple of men she had met online. Naturally, her parents became concerned.

"These people are 20 to 30 years old," said her father, Jim Stevens, "and she's a 15-year-old child."[1]

Even though Jamie had two very distraught parents, Mr. and Mrs. Stevens weren't about to just sit back and hope that Jamie would come home on her own. And they weren't going to simply depend on the police to do the searching for them. Instead, they took action on their own.

The first thing Jamie's parents did was to reach out to Jamie's friends and make them all aware of how concerned they were for Jamie's safety. They made sure that Jamie's friends knew that all they wanted was just to have her back home safely. This is a very important thing for the parents of a runaway to do. Because if parents, rather than showing love and concern, instead act angry and upset, threatening what they'll do when they find their child, friends of the child will likely be very reluctant to help, believing that perhaps the child had a good reason for running away.

Also, while it is important to show love and concern, there is another extremely important thing that the parents of runaway children need to do. Runaways with a large circle of friends at school; at church; at after-school activities; and, just as important, online will quite often keep in touch with these friends even after running away. In today's e-mail, MySpace, and Facebook society, keeping in touch is as simple as finding a computer. Therefore, parents need to reach out to these friends and not only show concern for their child's safety, but also ask these friends for their help in ensuring the child's safe return.

But Jamie's parents did something even more in their effort to locate her. They traced where the e-mail she had sent to her mother had come from (we will talk below about how to do this). Through this, Jamie's parents found that her e-mail had come from the Woodinville Public Library. Woodinville is a suburb of Seattle, about seven miles northwest of Redmond.

The real break in the search for Jamie, though, came because Jamie's mother and father had reached out to all of their daughter's friends and asked for their help. Consequently, these friends were also looking for Jamie. On November 3, 2009, one of these friends spotted Jamie at the library in Lynnwood, Washington, another suburb of Seattle. The friend saw Jamie on the computer there checking her e-mail account. The friend then called Jamie's mother, who notified the police. Officers found Jamie in a nearby park in the company of a twenty-year-old man.

"She was sorry she had not kept in touch with her family and friends and caused so much worry," Jamie's mother said. "She will be coming back home."[2]

In a similar story, the mother of a runaway girl, also from the Seattle area, suddenly received a telephone call from her daughter, who had run away from school in the company of two adults, a man and a woman. The daughter called her mother to assure her that she was all right.

The mother wasn't assured, however. Her home telephone system had caller ID, which displays the telephone number of callers, and so the mother did a Web search on the number her daughter had called from. To her horror, the mother found that the telephone number was connected to a website that promoted prostitution. The site, when the mother pulled it up, ran an advertisement for a "Sexy Puerto Rican with DDD Buttercups." The mother immediately notified the police, who went to the address of the website owner.

At that address, the police found several juvenile girls, including the woman's runaway daughter. The authorities arrested twenty-one-year-old Kendra Michon and charged her with Attempted Promoting Commercial Sexual Abuse of a Minor. Kendra claimed that she was simply starting up an escort service and that no sex would be involved, despite the ad on her website. The girls, however, told the police that they had been instructed to always ask if the customer was a police officer.

"The defendant was at least temporarily housing three other juveniles who are believed to be recruited for her 'escort business,'" said Senior Deputy Prosecutor Sean O'Donnell. "All of the girls are minors, three were reported missing as runaways."[3]

What these two incidents have in common is that in both cases the parents of runaways didn't just sit back and wait for the police or someone else to find their children. The parents themselves took an active role in the search, and they were successful in locating their runaway children.

While it would be nice to suppose that the police, when called by parents and notified of runaway children, would pull out all the stops and have a dozen or more of their best officers conduct an immediate search for the missing children, this just isn't going to happen. Unless parents can show that their children are in imminent danger of death or serious injury, the kind of search described above is not going to materialize. There are simply too many runaways every year and not enough police officers.

Also, practically speaking, it is simply not worth the manpower it would take for police departments to properly search for runaways. Statistics show that 95 percent of runaway children return home on their own within a few days or are located within a few weeks in some other way. So realistically, the police would be wasting their time in 95 percent of the cases if they tried to find all of the estimated two million runaway children every year.

Still, readers may wonder, what about the 5 percent of runaways (around 100,000 children yearly) who don't return home on their own in a few days or who aren't found within a few weeks in some other way? Who looks for them? The simple truth is that finding them is usually left up to the parents, as the following incidents show very clearly.

Nicholle Coppler, a fourteen-year-old, became unhappy about all the rules her parents had set for her at home. On May 15, 1999, while supposedly on her way to school, she instead ran away with an acquaintance named Glen Fryer, a man with a shady past. Krista Coppler, Nicholle's mother, reported her daughter's disappearance to the police department in Lima, Ohio, but wasn't happy at all with what she felt was a lack of response from them.

"I just think the police department botched the whole thing," she said.[4]

Deana Lauck, a juvenile investigator for the Lima Police Department responded, "Lima police take a report when a parent calls to report a runaway child. That doesn't mean police drop everything to look for that child. A heavy caseload and too few officers mean little can be done right away."[5] However, Lauck added that if a case has special circumstances, such as imminent danger, the police will likely get right on it.

Nicholle's mother has to this day never heard from or about her daughter. She and the police believe that Fryer knows what happened to Nicholle, but, after pleading no contest to a rape charge, Fryer committed suicide in prison without ever saying anything.

Reinforcing the Lima Police Department's stance on runaway children, Detective Sergeant Tom Wagner, head of the Las Vegas Metro's Missing Persons Unit, said that if it was his kid who ran away, "I wouldn't rely on just the police to do my investigation."[6]

Similarly, Debra Gwartney also received scant help from law enforcement when she reported two of her daughters as runaways. The trouble started when, following her divorce, Gwartney moved her four daughters from Tucson, Arizona, to Eugene, Oregon. Her daughters apparently didn't like the idea of relocating, and two of them ran away from home. Although Gwartney finally located her two daughters, she said she didn't get much help from the police.

"The police have no mandate to find runaways," said Gwartney. "I went to quite a few police stations and asked for help, and they all told me the same thing: We don't do that. Sorry."[7]

In a final example, the Phoenix Police Department website contains the following statement: "The Phoenix Police Department Missing Persons Investigators are very willing to assist you in finding [your] child. However, the primary responsibility for locating a runaway falls on the parent or guardian of the child."[8]

This is simply a reality of today's world that the parents of runaway children must accept. The major duty of finding their runaway children rests with them. There is simply too much crime and too few police to assign officers to look for runaways. I'm not saying that there aren't some smaller police departments that won't do an extensive and active search for runaways, because there are. In very small communities the police rarely receive runaway reports and can therefore justify an extensive search. For example, seventeen-year-old Theresa Meadows ran away from her home in Mechanicsville, Virginia (population 30,464), in 2004. The Hanover County Sheriff's Department, which patrols the Mechanicsville area, receives only about fifty missing person cases every year, and Theresa's was one of only three that remained unsolved. As a result, Sheriff's Investigator Dave Klisz worked relentlessly to solve it, following up on and then rechecking every lead, month after month and then year after year. Finally, after five years, he did solve it. He found Theresa living in South Carolina under an assumed name.

"It was a very good ending," said Detective Klisz.[9]

While this is an example of great police work, it is a rare case, and a kind that is usually confined to small police departments. Even large police departments, however, while usually not conducting this type of search, will still distribute information about runaway children to their officers, who might encounter the children while on patrol or during other investigations. Also, parents of runaway children can usually get the officers in any size police department to assist them if they can come up with viable clues as to their children's location, but the parents must conduct the initial search for these clues. To expect a police department in any sizable community, with hundreds or more likely thousands of reported runaways, to initiate a search for every runaway child simply isn't realistic. There just isn't the necessary manpower.

However, as I said above, just because the police won't conduct an initial extensive search for runaway children doesn't mean they can't be of any help. If parents can provide the police with their runaway children's location, the police will usually go pick the children up. Also, if parents can provide the police with some good clues about the location of their children, the police will also usually follow up on these clues. And if, as in the incident above concerning the "escort service," parents can show the police that their runaway children are in danger, officers will most certainly follow up on it.

The point I'm making is that the parents of runaway children shouldn't just report their children to the authorities and then simply sit back and wait to hear from them or wait for the children to return on their own. This is extremely important because runaways, even if gone for only a short time, can still become involved in some very harmful and dangerous activities. So it is vital that parents begin a search for their runaway children as soon as they realize they are gone.

Before we discuss what should be done once parents realize that their children have run away from home, there are some things parents can do beforehand that will make finding their runaway children much easier. These measures will also prove helpful for parents in other situations involving their missing children, such as abductions or accidents away from home.

1. At least once every two or three months, parents should take several good photographs of their children, including profiles, and also shoot several minutes of video. Children can change quickly as they grow up, and parents will need good-quality photographs to put on a missing child poster or to give to the news media in the event their children disappear.

2. Parents should take their children to the local police department and have their fingerprints and a DNA sample taken. Some police

departments are now even doing iris scanning on children. The police will not keep these pieces of identification, but instead give them to the parents, who should store them in a safe, but readily available, place.

3. A very worthwhile piece of advice for parents is to keep a list of all their children's characteristics that make them unique, such as scars, birthmarks, dental work, medical conditions, handicaps, and so on. This list can come in very handy because parents will likely be under tremendous stress and not thinking clearly when they discover their children are missing.

4. Parents need to know who all of their children's friends are. Parents need to know and record names, ages, addresses, telephone numbers, e-mail addresses, and screen names. When children mention a new friend, parents should always be certain that they have this person on their list. This is not being intrusive. This is simply good parenting. I was always amazed as a police officer how little most parents knew about their children, and how much they wish they had known when an emergency arose.

5. Whether children are a runaway threat or not, parents must closely monitor their children's Internet activities. What websites do they visit? What chat rooms? Who are they talking with on the computer? What are their passwords and screen names? Sadly, many parents who didn't monitor their children's computer activities have found out too late that the world is full of sexual predators. These predators used to have to go out into the world to find their victims, but now can find thousands and thousands of them on their computer. Unfortunately, most children are naive and trusting, and will believe whatever a person on the computer tells them. As a result, thousands of runaways every year leave home to go meet someone they have been talking with on the computer, who often turns out to be a child sexual predator.

Again, keeping a check on children like this is not being intrusive, but simply good parenting. I and most other police officers have spoken with many parents who wished too late that they had done this kind of good parenting. Allowing children to have unsupervised access to the Internet is like turning them loose in a large city. There are many interesting things to see, but there are also many predators lying in wait for them.

"With so much social media out there, it's just not that plausible to rely on the schools or anyone else in the community to monitor all of the popular sites," said Dan Claassen, a police officer who runs mycyberguardian.org. "It's ultimately up to the parents to be responsible and to be aware of what kind of communication their children are having online."[10]

To assist parents in keeping an eye on their children's computer activities, there are software programs, such as Spector Pro, that parents can purchase and load onto their computer. These programs record everything children do on the computer. Using these programs, parents can pull up e-mails, both sides of chat messaging, and the various websites their children have visited. In addition, these programs can perform keystroke recording and also allow parents to enter "danger" words. When any of these words turn up during their children's computer activities the program alerts the parents. But a word of caution: in order to use these programs effectively, parents must know online lingo and abbreviations or they won't understand what their children are talking about. To remedy this, parents can visit www.NetSmartz. org for the latest in computer lingo and abbreviations.

6. The Greyhound Bus System has a program that provides free rides home to runaway children. Called the Greyhound Home Free Program, this project operates in partnership with the National Runaway Switchboard. "Greyhound has stepped forward to help reunite runaway children with their families," said Lora Thomas, previously the Executive Director of the National Runaway Switchboard. "Through Home Free, we can help runaways who want to return home but just don't have the means to do so."[11] To obtain a ticket, a runaway simply has to call the Runaway Switchboard. Wise parents should somehow make their children aware of this program.

7. If parents feel there is a good possibility that their children may become runaways sometime in the near future, it might be worthwhile for these parents to look into the Child Shield Program at 1-520-297-8881 or at www.childshieldusa.com. For a fee, this program will take care of printing and distributing missing child posters, duplicating video tapes, and sending these items to police departments, media out-

lets, and missing children organizations. The program also has an array of other services available that should be investigated by concerned parents.

We will close out this section with an example of how knowledgeable parents could have stopped a runaway incident from occurring. The parents in the incident below certainly wish that they had been aware of who their daughter had been talking with on the computer, and especially what they had been talking about.

The fifteen-year-old daughter of Brian and Elise Pringle seemed to be a healthy, well-adjusted young lady. Her parents had no idea she was corresponding over her computer with a teenage boy in North Carolina. One night in 2007 they all went to bed in Juneau, Alaska, a seemingly happy family. The next morning, the parents awoke to find their daughter gone. Where did she go?

Apparently, she went to the ticket counter at Alaska Airlines with a handful of one- and five-dollar bills and asked to purchase an airline ticket to North Carolina. The airline sold her the ticket without asking any questions or apparently checking for identification, and she boarded the airplane.

"She went to the airline, and at that point in time purchased her ticket in denominations of ones and fives at the actual ticket counter," the runaway's mother said. "I was flabbergasted because she looks 15 years old, she is 15 years old."[12]

Alaska Airlines and the Transportation Security Administration (TSA), when questioned by the news media, attempted to justify their actions. Alaska Airlines said that their policy on unaccompanied minors allows children thirteen and over to travel by themselves. The TSA said that they only require identification for passengers older than eighteen. Yet neither of these organizations could explain how these rules applied when no one apparently asked the runaway girl to prove how old she was or asked why she was traveling alone.

"A 15-year-old walking up to a window and having cash and having no ID should set off bells with the airline to further check this out," said former FBI agent Brad Garrett.[13]

Fortunately, the Pringles were able to alert the police at the airplane's first stop about their daughter's status. The authorities in Seattle picked her up and returned her home.

Before we get into a list of the things parents should do in the first hours and even days after a child has run away from home, there is one crucial thing that they should immediately, and without fail, do, and that is to notify the local police. Amazingly, according to the U.S. Department of Justice report *Juvenile Runaways*, parents report only about 20 percent of all runaways to the police.[14] Why? There are a number of reasons. Some parents, researchers have found, don't report runaways because they are certain the children will return soon. Others don't report because they are angry at the children and glad that they are gone. In far too many cases, parents don't report runaways because they are embarrassed to have to admit family problems to the police. And finally, a number of parents don't report their children as runaways because they fear that involving the police will give their children a record that will follow them for life.

But not reporting runaway children to the police is extremely unwise. I know I said above that the police will likely be of little help in the initial search, but too many bad things can happen to children out in the world on their own. And while the police may not conduct an extensive search, they will act if they encounter runaway children during their investigations. For all the parents know, the police may have already encountered their runaway children and know where they are, or the police may run into the children in the near future, but they won't do anything if they don't know that the children are runaways. Also, if parents do turn up clues as to the location of their runaway children, and these parents haven't reported the children as missing yet, the police won't be able to act, or at least act quickly.

For parents wanting to report a child as a runaway, the local police department will usually send an officer to the child's home, but occasionally parents will need to go to the police station in order to file a missing person report. A number of states have adopted laws similar to Patricia's Law in New Jersey, a statute named after Patricia Viola, who disappeared in 2001. This law requires, among other things, that the police take without delay any report of a missing person, and does not allow the police to refuse to take a missing person report for any reason.

There are certain things that parents should have with them when they report a child as a runaway. The first thing they will need is at least one recent photograph that depicts how the child really looks, not a staged photograph or a flattering one, but a realistic one. Readers would be surprised how often parents want to report a child as a runaway, but have or bring no recent picture. Detective Sergeant Tom Wagner, head of the Las Vegas Metro's Missing Persons Unit, told a reporter that in 40 percent of runaway cases, parents don't bring in a photograph.[15]

Also, parents should have a biographical sketch of their runaway child with all of the physical attributes that help identify him or her, such as height, weight, hair color and style, wears glasses, wears braces, birthmarks, scars, and so on. Along with this, parents should be certain to tell the officers about any serious medical conditions the child may have, such as asthma or diabetes. This could change the child's case from ordinary to high priority.

In addition, the police will need the names, addresses, and telephone numbers of all of the runaway's friends. Helpful too is a list of places the runaway child frequents, along with suspected destinations and companions if the parents know of any. Finally, parents should tell the police about any previous runaway episodes and their outcome, as children will often tend to follow the same pattern. Of course, accomplishing much of this will be a lot easier if parents follow my advice above and do it ahead of time.

If a runaway child has a cellular telephone, parents should be certain to give this information to the police. A youth's cell phone can show the police exactly where he or she is. In October 2009, for example, a fourteen-year-old boy with Asperger's syndrome ran away from his home in Clackamas County, Oregon. His mother, naturally distraught, contacted the police and told them that her son was a runaway with a disability, and that he had taken his cell phone with him. Police later discovered that the child had apparently used his mother's credit card information to purchase an airline ticket to Chicago. The police contacted AT&T and had them put a trace on the cell phone. AT&T quickly discovered that the phone was at O'Hare International Airport in Chicago. The Clackamas County Sheriff's Department notified the O'Hare Airport Police, who soon found the boy in the baggage area. Apparently, the youngster had been corresponding with a girl in Chicago over his computer and had decided to visit her.

In addition, if a runaway child has a car or other vehicle, parents should be certain to give the police all the information they have about it. The police can then put out a "Be on the Lookout" order for it.

Parents who have previously had their children fingerprinted or have had DNA samples taken should of course give these to the police. These will be necessary in the event the police need to identify children found in another jurisdiction. The police may also ask parents for the children's dental records.

Along with giving the police what information they have, parents should, if the police request it, also grant them access to a runaway child's medical and school records, and to the child's e-mail and other Internet activities. If a police department is this interested in finding a runaway child, parents certainly don't want to discourage them. Parents should also give the police their child's computer passwords and screen names.

One of the most important things, though, that the parents of runaway children must do is to be totally honest with the police about the possible reasons a child has run away. Knowing the reasons can help the police in any investigation of clues that may turn up. Many families don't like the idea of having to air dirty laundry, but not having all of the facts will only hamper the police. If a child is involved in drugs or other illegal activities, for example, parents must tell the police about this because then their drug enforcement officers can also be on the lookout for the child. Believe me, whatever parents tell the police will not shock them. No family is perfect, and the police realize this.

Also extremely important, parents must be certain that the police department enters their runaway child's name into the FBI's National Crime Information Center (NCIC) computer system. Parents should ask the police for the NCIC case number, and record it. This will not give a runaway child a police record, but can be crucial to finding the child because every police agency in the United States has access to this computer system. Therefore, no matter where a child turns up in the United States, the local police will know that he or she is a runaway.

The Adam Walsh Child Protection and Safety Act (Public Law No. 109-248) mandates that entry must be made by law enforcement into NCIC's Missing Person File within two hours of receipt of a report of a missing or abducted child. Yet police departments still don't always do this. A study reported in the *New York Times* found that 16 percent of runaways reported to the police are never entered into NCIC.[16] If parents find that for some reason the local police department will not do this, these parents should immediately contact the local FBI office and ask them to do it. It is much too important a step to ignore. A report by the U.S. Department of Justice, for example, tells of the case of a mentally retarded runaway boy who spent many months in a children's center because the police hadn't entered his information into NCIC, and so the local authorities couldn't find out where he was missing from.[17]

"Shockingly, many runaway children are missing not only from their homes, but also from the very database meant to help law enforcement officers find them," said Congresswoman Carolyn Maloney about the failure of many police departments to enter runaway children into NCIC. "If no one knows that a child is missing, that child is unlikely to be found."[18]

Parents should also be certain that the local police department sends the information about their runaway child to the state missing children clearinghouse, and also be certain that the police department distributes the information to its officers so that they can be on the lookout for the runaway child. In big police departments particularly, information can often get pigeon-holed and not reach the ones who can make the most use of it.

After contacting the local police department about a runaway child, parents should additionally contact the local sheriff's department, the state police, and police departments in adjoining jurisdictions. While it would be nice to assume that all of these police departments share information on runaway children, unfortunately this doesn't always happen.

Even though, as I said earlier, the police will likely be of little or no help in the initial search for a runaway, I want to stress again how important it is for parents to notify the police about a runaway child. It is important because if parents can turn up clues concerning the location of a runaway child, or if the parents are able to give the police some tangible items that will assist in the search for a runaway child, the police can, as in the incidents below, be of great assistance.

In February 2008, a twelve-year-old boy and his thirteen-year-old sister ran away from home in Walhalla, South Carolina. When they left they took their parents' car. The police found the runaways the next evening at a gas station in Bethlehem, Georgia. How did the police locate the children?

The parents, when reporting their children as runaways, provided the police with the number of a cell phone the children had taken with them. The parents also informed the officers that the children had taken, along with the car and cell phone, an ATM card. The police found that the children had used the ATM card near Augusta, Georgia, and then began tracking their movements through their cell phone.

In another incident, this one in August 2010, the Fairfax County Police arrested Joshua J. Gessler, an attorney with Arnold & Porter, one of Washington, D.C.'s most prestigious law firms. They charged Gessler with one count of Producing Child Pornography and five counts of Possessing Child Pornography. The police were alerted to Gessler through the mother of a fifteen-year-old runaway who had allowed the police to have access to her daughter's e-mail account after she had found suspicious and disturbing activity on it. Using this information, according to news reports, the police tracked several e-mails containing sexually explicit pictures of the runaway to a computer owned by Gessler. The runaway girl reportedly admitted to the police that Gessler had given her $300 to pose for the pictures and that he had told her he wanted to bring along bondage items to use in these photographs.[19]

One final bit of advice about dealing with the police: Don't allow them to brush you off. One thing I learned from thirty-eight years in law enforcement is that the squeaky wheel usually does get the grease. If parents don't think the police are doing enough, especially if they have given the police information that could locate a runaway child, parents should go to the next level of supervision, and continue to do so until they get results.

However, to make this a fair discussion, before we leave the subject of dealing with the police there are a number of legitimate reasons why the police don't want to take reports or be bothered with runaways. One of these reasons is that many communities have no place to take runaway children, and so the police are stuck with them until the parents come to pick them up, which can often be some time. Also, looking for and picking up runaways is just one more task and a lot more paperwork in a job that has ever increasing demands for police involvement in more serious public safety threats. And finally, runaway cases can be frustrating because often the children don't want to go home, and the parents don't want them to come home, which means that the children will likely just run away again.

Still, regardless of whether or not the police like runaway cases, it is in the parents' best interest to always involve the police. So, once parents have made a runaway report to the police, they should then keep in touch with whoever at the police department is in charge of their child's case. This is important because the police department may turn up information that doesn't mean anything to them but does to the parents. And if the officer doesn't return their calls, parents should contact the officer's supervisor.

Following notification to the police, there are a number of important things that the parents of a runaway child should do in the first hours and days after discovering that a child is missing:

1. Although there are few fears more paralyzing than a missing child, parents must still try to remain calm so that they can think clearly. Most parents are stunned the first time they find that one of their children has run away from home, and will often have no context with which to respond to the situation, and so they flounder with indecision. Some parents also become angry and hostile. These states of mind cloud clear thinking, and in order to conduct a proper search for a missing child, clear thinking is essential.

2. Parents should immediately start a notebook and write down everything they do in their attempt to find a runaway child. Information written on loose scraps of paper can too easily get lost. A notebook will keep parents from doubling back because they will know where they've been and who they've talked to. In the initial stress of finding that a child is missing it is easy to get confused and not remember if someone has been called or if something has been done. In addition, parents should write down the names and badge numbers of all the police officers they deal with, and also document everyone talked to concerning a runaway child and the content of the conversation. This will come in handy if the search for a runaway child runs into weeks or months, because parents will want to check back with many people for updates and progress reports. Finally, parents should write down any questions they have for law enforcement or others. In the rush and stress that accompanies parents finding that a child has run away, these questions can easily be forgotten.

3. If parents believe there is any possibility at all that a missing child is not a runaway, but instead has been abducted, they should not enter their child's room or touch any of the child's property. Crimes today can be solved through the minutest of evidence. With the new DNA technology available, a single strand of hair or drop of saliva can lead the police to a perpetrator. And parents should particularly not examine their child's computer, which to experts can produce extremely valuable evidence. If parents do disturb a child's room or touch his or her property, they can very easily destroy this evidence.

4. Many parents of runaways want an Amber Alert issued for their child. Amber Alert is a national program that uses news media outlets, electronic highways signs, and other methods to alert the public to an abducted child in danger. This program has had phenomenal success in locating abducted children and returning them home safely. Unfortunately, most runaways don't fit the necessary requirements for an Amber Alert, since most have left home voluntarily and are not yet in danger. If the Amber Alert system did post alerts for runaways there would quickly be so many alerts that the public would no longer pay any attention to them and the system would become useless.

5. If parents, on the other hand, are certain that their child is a runaway, not an abduction victim, they should check their child's computer to see who he or she has been talking with recently. If parents aren't computer savvy, they should find someone who is. E-mail on a runaway child's computer could give evidence of a planned meeting between the child and someone he or she has met on the computer, as will conversations in chat rooms and texting. Also, parents should see if their child has recently accessed MapQuest or some other mapping site for a possible destination. In addition to examining their child's computer, parents should also check their child's cell phone. Finally, children who run away from home usually have little or no resources. Therefore, for the first few weeks at least, they will often use the family cell phone, e-mail accounts, and so on. As we will see below, parents can many times use this fact to locate their runaway children.

6. Along with the computer and other personal electronic devices, parents should also search for letters, diary entries, maps, and any other clues as to where their child may have gone and with whom.

7. Parents should search their child's desk at school and also check his or her locker for clues. Interestingly, it has been found in some cases that even though a child has run away from home, he or she will still go to school for the security of companionship, especially if he or she is staying with friends.

8. At any major crime scene one of the things the police always do is canvass the surrounding neighborhood for witnesses to the crime. It is surprising how often the police find witnesses who either didn't realize the significance of what they saw or didn't want to get involved at the scene for fear of being labeled a snitch. Since the police likely won't do this in a runaway case, parents need to. They should knock on every door for several blocks surrounding the last place their child was known to be and ask if the residents have seen their child or know where he or she went.

9. It is important for parents to determine whether their child's running away was spontaneous or planned. As might be imagined, spontaneous runaways are often easier to find since they have made no plans and will usually have little resources. Because of this, they

will often seek out friends or family for help. But also in spontaneous runaway cases, parents should look in vacant homes in the neighborhood. Children will many times know a way in and may not have any other place to stay. Additionally, parents should check homes in the neighborhood up for sale but not occupied, all homeless shelters in the area, the bus station (where people can sleep out of the cold and not be conspicuous), and abandoned buildings. Also, children who have impulsively run away will many times try to sneak back into their home at night or when the parents are at work in order to get some of their property.

If parents find instead that their child has planned the running away through the taking of important personal items, such as a cell phone, iPod, clothing, and particularly money, the child can be harder to find because he or she has likely arranged transportation and usually has a place to stay. If it is a planned runaway, parents should try to determine, if possible, the child's plan. For girls with older boyfriends, for example, parents usually need only to find the boyfriend in order to find their daughter. Parents should also check to see if their child has done map searches on the Internet; has visited airline, bus, or train websites; or has been talking to someone unknown to the parents over the Internet. Finally, sometimes a child's destination can be determined by discovering exactly what property he or she has taken (e.g., summer clothing and beach wear, etc.).

10. Boyfriends or girlfriends of runaways should be one of the first sources parents check. If they are also missing, it is likely the two have run away together. If not missing, they will be more likely than anyone else to know what is going on. Also, check with previous boyfriends and girlfriends. Parents never know what might have rekindled.

11. Along with romantic interests, parents should also talk with all of their runaway children's other friends. If parents have made a list, as I recommended, this will be much simpler.

"In the case of a missing or runaway child, the obvious first step is to interview the child's friends *without* a parent standing by," Leigh Hearon, who runs Leigh Hearon Investigative Services in Seattle, told me. "Most often, runaways stay with friends, and they can be quite ingenious about hiding their presence right under their friend's parent's roof."[20]

However, parents of a runaway shouldn't just talk to their child's friends but also to the friends' parents. The parents of a runaway child's friends may have heard their children talking about the runaway, or may have seen the child and not know that he or she was a runaway. Often runaways will do what is called "couch surfing" for several weeks after running away, meaning they will sleep on friends' couches until they wear out this option and must find other sleeping arrangements.

Another important thing for parents to inquire about is whether any friends of their runaway children are also missing. If so, it is very possible that they have run away together. The other parents may have important information about the runaway children's location.

Also, when talking with anyone about a runaway child, parents should do what the police do when finishing up an interview, and that is to ask the person if he or she knows anyone else who might have information. This will often lead the police to other sources of information they wouldn't have known about, and it can work for parents too.

12. Parents should tell all of their children's friends that, if they want, they can pass on any information they have to the National Runaway Switchboard, which will then pass the information on to the parent. This way no one will know where the information came from.

13. Along with their children's friends, parents should also talk with neighbors. Do they know anything? Have they seen anything suspicious? Additionally, parents should check with coworkers if their runaway children are employed. Occasionally, runaway children, because of a lack of resources, will continue to work. Also, parents should find out if their children have a paycheck coming. They will likely come back for it.

14. Talking with a runaway child's teachers, coaches, classmates, and youth group leaders can also occasionally provide useful information. Do they know where the child may have gone? Have they noticed any recent changes in the child? Has the child suddenly developed new friends? Parents should also talk to members of any clubs their child

belonged to, and to any children they can find who share their child's interests and hobbies.

15. Often, a good place to gain clues as to a runaway child's plans is any location the child was known to frequent and hang out. Parents should talk to everyone they can find there, and not forget to go back and talk to people who work on different shifts.

16. The parents of a runaway child should also call and talk with ex-spouses and ex-in-laws. These individuals may not know that the child is a runaway but know where he or she is. Runaway children will often stay, at least at first, with extended family.

17. If a week passes by with no information, parents should call back all of the people they have already contacted to see if they have heard anything new. In addition to possibly gaining new information, this lets these people know how concerned the parents are, which can make them more likely to call if they do hear something.

18. The parents of runaway children should have caller ID installed on their telephone system. This way, if their children do call, the parents will know the number called from. Often, runaway children, after being gone for several days or weeks, will call home, wanting to see what attitude their parents have about their disappearance and a possible return. Parents might also want to consider having Call Trace and/or Call Return installed. In addition, parents should leave a message for their children on the answering machine. They should make certain their children know that coming home is an option. Children can quickly regret their decision to run away, but be unsure about how to negotiate a return.

19. Parents of runaway children should make up a missing child poster. On it, they should put a full face picture and, if they have it, a profile picture of the runaway child. They shouldn't, however, pick a picture because it is flattering, but instead choose one that truly depicts the runaway child. Also, the flier should include all descriptive data that would help anyone who sees the poster identify the child. This includes the color of hair and eyes, height and weight, date of birth, gender, date of disappearance, circumstances of disappearance, and anyone the child may be in the company of. Also included on the poster should be any specific identifiers such as birthmarks, scars, braces, glasses, pierc-

ings, and anything else that sets the child apart. But it's very important that parents not forget to list any medical conditions, such as diabetes, asthma, depression, special medications, and so on. The telephone number, including the area code, of the police department handling the runaway child's case should be in bold print. (Without an area code, anyone spotting the runaway child outside the local area will not be able to notify anyone.) Parents probably should not put their own telephone number or address on the flier because this can set them up for hoaxes, crank calls, and scams. Finally, parents might want to put a note of concern on the poster so that the child knows he or she is missed and loved. A sample missing child flier can be found in the U.S. Department of Justice book *When Your Child Is Missing: A Family Survival Guide*. Readers can access this document at www.ojjdp.gov/pubs/childismissing/contents.html or order it from 1-800-851-3420.

20. The missing child posters, once made up, should be distributed everywhere children may congregate, and especially at any places the runaway child liked to hang out. If the runaway child is still in the area, he or she will want to continue social interactions and may go to these places. Parents should also attempt to persuade local groups such as churches, charitable organizations, and boy and girl scouts to assist them in distributing the fliers. Several important places to be certain to leave one of these posters are at all local hospitals, transportation centers, local motels, and particularly at any truck stops in the area. Truckers regularly cross the country and could spot the runaway child trying to hitch a ride.

Above all, parents must be persuasive or find someone who is persuasive to distribute the missing child fliers, and attempt to get one posted in every heavy traffic area possible. Parents should also e-mail a copy of their poster to everyone on their e-mail list and request that these individuals forward it to all of the people on their list. Parents should also send a copy to everyone on their child's e-mail list.

Parents must additionally send or deliver a missing child poster to every immediate-care medical center in the region. If runaway children become injured or sick, they may want to avoid hospitals and instead seek medical help at one of these locations. Parents should also send a copy of their missing-child flier to every runaway shelter in the area. If their runaway children have worn out the hospitality of their friends, they may seek help at a shelter. The Runaway and Homeless Youth Act, a federal law, requires states with runaway shelters that receive federal funds to develop procedures for the shelter staff to notify parents within twenty-four to seventy-two hours of a youth's admission to the shelter.[21] With a poster in their possession, this will be much easier.

On January 19, 1996, President Clinton signed an Executive Memorandum requiring all federal agencies to post fliers for missing children in their buildings. The National Center for Missing and Exploited Children at www.missingkids.com or 1-800-843-5678 coordinates this program, which can possibly bring crucially needed information from someone viewing these fliers. Check with the Center to see if your child qualifies.

Finally, if parents can arrange it, they should be certain that the vice squads of all police departments nearby or where they suspect their children might have gone to receive a copy of the missing child poster. These officers may have seen the runaway children during prostitution sweeps. Often, the success of finding runaways depends on how many people are aware of the children's status and are looking for them. The more eyes looking, the more successful parents will be.

21. A very important organization for the parents of a runaway child to contact is the National Center for Missing and Exploited Children (NCMEC). Parents should send this organization one of their missing child posters, which NCMEC will then distribute to their over 26,000 contacts across the nation. This organization also has a vast array of other services and contacts that can assist the parents of a runaway child. In addition, NCMEC has over 125,000 hits every day on their website, where visitors will see the missing child poster.

22. In addition, videos of a runaway child can be posted on the YouTube Missing Children's Channel. This resource can be accessed at www.youtube.com/DontYouForgetAboutMe.

23. For runaways such as Francisco Hernandez, discussed in chapter 1, who are prone to running away and have disabilities that make them especially vulnerable, parents should consider purchasing clothing with GPS tracking devices hidden in them. These clothing items can include jackets, shoes, etc. With these devices, a missing child can

be found within minutes. One of the biggest suppliers of these hidden GPS devices is the Zoombak Company (www.zoombak.com).

24. Parents of runaway children should check with any cult awareness centers in their area. Cults often recruit runaway children. If parents do find that their children may be in a cult, they should see my book *Deadly Cults: The Crimes of True Believers* for advice about what to do.[22]

25. An important fact parents should be aware of is that children occasionally run away from home in order to follow their favorite band. If parents believe this may be the case, then a schedule of the band's tour can pinpoint the child's location.

26. For runaway children who have a car, parents should check local towing and impound lots. Also, parents should make the police aware of any automated toll payment features in the car, such as EZ Pass. The vehicle's direction of travel can be tracked through this.

27. Any mention of a runaway child in the news media is worth hundreds of posters. Consequently, if parents have any contacts in the news media, they should attempt to get a mention of their child. Also, parents shouldn't forget local weeklies and community newspapers.

28. While parents may not have suspected this, they should check all local abortion clinics for runaway teenage girls. A young girl may have become a runaway because she is pregnant and doesn't know how to tell her parents. The same advice holds for the parents of a boy who has run away with his girlfriend.

29. Parents might want to consider offering a reward for information about a runaway child. However, parents who decide to do this should seek legal advice first because this can become a legally binding contract. Also, parents should be certain that the reward can be claimed anonymously so that the runaway's friends will be motivated to give up information.

30. A worthwhile project for the parents of runaway children is to research the laws in their state concerning runaways. In some states, for example, running away from home is a status offense (which means it is a crime that applies only to juveniles and that the police can pick up and hold a child for it), and in some states the police have very little authority. Harboring a runaway in some states is a criminal offense and

in some it is not. In some states runaway shelters (not receiving federal assistance) must notify parents if their children come there. The laws in a parent's state affecting runaways are important because they will make a difference concerning what the police can do if they find a runaway child. Also, knowing the laws can allow parents to use them as leverage if they believe someone may be harboring their runaway child.

31. In an anecdote earlier in this chapter I told readers about how the parents of a runaway child had traced her e-mails to a local library computer. How did they do this? There are a number of computer software programs that parents can use to trace e-mails, such as eMail-TrackerPro and VisualRoute. The sheriff's department in Jefferson County, Kansas, for example, recently used these programs to trace an e-mail from a Kansas runaway to a specific computer in Utah. Using this information, they alerted the Utah authorities, who picked up the runaway. With some of these software programs, if parents reply to an e-mail from their runaway child, the program will tell the parents exactly where the reply goes to.

32. There are also computer software applications, such as Accu-Tracking, that will allow parents to track the location of a cell phone. Many parents use these software programs for children who drive the family car. The application will tell where the car is (as long as the child has the cell phone along), the direction it is heading, and its speed. Parents of runaways can use these programs to track the whereabouts a child who has taken along a cell phone.

33. If runaway children call home collect, parents should be sure to ask the operator where the call originated from.

34. Within a few days of children running away, parents should call the National Runaway Switchboard at 1-800-RUNAWAY (786-2929) to see if their children have left a message for them. Parents should also leave a message for their children on the switchboard so that they will know that coming home is an option. The National Runaway Switchboard, besides being a message center, is also a resource center that many runaway children in need of food and shelter will turn to. In 2008, the National Runaway Switchboard received over 114,000 calls.

"Everything we do at the National Runaway Switchboard focuses on keeping runaway and at-risk youth safe and off the streets," Maureen Blaha, executive director of the National Runaway Switchboard, told me. "To that end, our number one priority when a youth calls 1-800-RUNAWAY or connects with us using our live chat service through 1800RUNAWAY.org is to make sure their safety isn't in jeopardy. We help them get to a shelter or other safe haven by tapping into our database of more than 13,000 resources throughout the country, which assist our frontline team members in successfully connecting runaway youth with help and safety."[23]

35. Parents of runaway children need to check to see if any of their credit or ATM cards are missing, and watch for any unauthorized transactions on them. In addition, if a runaway child has a bank account, parents should check for withdrawals. Also, parents need to examine telephone bills for any unexplained long-distance calls.

36. Finally, as we saw in the first incident in this chapter, social networking can be so important to today's youth that even though they may run away from home they continue to take part in their social network. According to the U.S. Department of Education, 23 percent of nursery school children in the United States use the Internet, 32 percent of kindergarteners, and 80 percent of high schoolers.[24] Consequently, parents of runaway children should closely monitor all social networks that their children were involved in before running away because the children will often stay involved with them afterward. Also, the runaway's friends on the social network can be very useful sources of information. As the following incidents show, parents of runaway children can often use social networking to their advantage.

Rachel Buyher's sixteen-year-old daughter ran away from home on November 3, 2010. Buyher filed a report with the police and then waited. But when after several days nothing had happened, she decided to take over the search herself. She used Facebook to post a picture of her daughter with a request that anyone who knew of her whereabouts to contact the police. She also requested that others on Facebook cross-post her daughter's picture and information.

"I had no idea the response I was going to get," said Buyher.[25]

To her surprise, Buyher received thousands of messages from people offering their support. She even received a message from a Massachusetts police officer who offered his help in the search.

On November 8, 2010, the authorities called Buyher and told her that they had received an anonymous tip on where to find her daughter. When the police went there they did indeed locate the runaway girl. Buyher believes absolutely that someone on Facebook saw her plea for help and called the police.

In a similar incident, Kelsey Ray, a sixteen-year-old girl from Missoula, Montana, ran away from home in early 2010. Apparently, she felt betrayed and devastated by the recent separation of her parents.

"She had not been in trouble before," said Monica Ray, her mother. "She was really hurting and we didn't know."[26]

When Kelsey's mother called the police about her daughter's disappearance, they reportedly told her that they didn't have the resources to search for a runaway and that Kelsey would likely return home on her own anyway. This was despite the fact that Monica believed Kelsey was headed for Seattle in the company of two teenage boys with criminal records. Regardless of what the police told her, waiting for Kelsey to return on her own wasn't an option for Monica, and so she set out to find Kelsey herself.

Monica placed a missing person poster on Facebook and Twitter. Within two days, she found that over 60,000 people had responded by clicking on the poster. The authorities soon began receiving tips that Kelsey had been seen in the Seattle area. The police then began tracing text messages Kelsey sent on her cell phone.

On June 7, 2010, the police in Kirkland, Washington, a suburb of Seattle, contacted Kelsey's mother and told her that they had located her daughter. The sheriff of Mineral County, Montana, issued a statement thanking "the many, and I do mean many, people who provided support via the Facebook page dedicated to finding Kelsey. This was social networking at its finest."[27]

In some cases, information on the social networking site itself can help find a runaway. In Connecticut in 2009, a young girl with seemingly no reason to run away from home disappeared with another girl. They traveled to New York City and ended up playing the guitar and begging for money on the street. One of the girls eventually used her Facebook page to post an update of her status. Upon request of the police, Facebook provided them with the Internet server used, through which the police found that the computer utilized to make the update was in a boarding house in New York City. Going to the address of the boarding house, the police found the runaway girls.

So far in this chapter we have talked about all the things parents should do before their children run away from home and about what they should do in the first hours, days, and weeks after their children have run away. But suppose months or even a year or more has passed since children have run away, and no one is looking for them any longer. Is there anything parents can do? Yes, there is.

1. First off, parents should never give up hope. Just because a runaway child has been missing for a long time doesn't mean that he or she will never be found. As an example, in September 2010 the police in Henderson, Kentucky, located Jamie Lee Owen, who had run away from her home in September of 2009. The authorities charged twenty-seven-year-old Joshua Guthrie with Felony Custodial Interference after they found seventeen-year-old Jamie hiding in one of Joshua's closets.

"Some activity on Facebook and MySpace led us to believe that she was okay, just that we couldn't find her," said Sergeant Steve Gibson of the Henderson Police Department.[28] The police had received a tip that Jamie might be at Joshua's house, and when they went there and talked with Joshua, he eventually admitted that Jamie was there. "We wanted to check to see if she'd been held against her will for a year, which wasn't the case," said Sergeant Gibson.[29]

Uncertainty and despair are the worst enemies of a parent's emotional well-being. Parents of runaway children should always keep in mind that missing children have been found alive and well months and even years after disappearing. Never give up hope.

2. One of the most important things to do with runaway cases that are months or even years old is to keep the cases alive by sponsoring events that will tie into the runaway children and will also attract the

attention of the news media. Parents must keep the runaways' names and pictures out in the public eye so that anyone who sees the children will realize that they are runaways and consequently notify the police. As I said above, often the success of finding runaway children depends on how many people know the children are missing and are therefore looking for them.

But to accomplish this, parents must have a "media hook" to get coverage about their runaway children. A few ideas for this include sponsoring a drive to have children fingerprinted by the local police, or sponsoring a youth fair where child safety is taught. Parents might also want to consider organizing a benefit auction for missing children. In addition, November is National Runaway Prevention Month and May 25 is International Missing Children Day. Sponsoring events on these days can bring attention to a parent's runaway child.

Along with the above, parents can also try to persuade a local athlete or other celebrity to endorse the cause of missing children. These individuals can garner much more publicity than a parent alone can, and parents can then include their own children's information in this endorsement campaign. Another idea is to have pin-on buttons made up with the runaway children's pictures on them or have pictures of the runaway children put on helium balloons that the parents can release in different parts of their area. By the way, if it can be managed, a spot on a television program such as *America's Most Wanted* is worth 100,000 posters.

3. Although few parents may realize it, direct mail services such as Valassis reach millions of homes every week. These are the small magazines sent through the mail that are made up totally of advertisements and coupons. Valassis has a "Have You Seen Me?" program that the parents of a long-term runaway should look into. A recent mailing that came to my house in December 2010 listed children who had been missing since 2005.

4. The May 2009 issue of the *North County Times* contained an article about how the Lake Elsinore Outlet Mall south of Los Angeles maintains a large video sign at its entrance.[30] On this sign the mall displayed pictures of missing children for International Missing Children Day on May 25. This is the kind of publicity parents of long-term

runaway children need. Of course, to be of the most practical value, parents must use an age-progression picture, since the children will likely have changed in the time they have been gone. These, as we will talk about below, can be obtained from NCMEC. Regardless, a spot like this could be a real help to the parents of runaway children since thousands of people a day will see these signs and could remember seeing a missing child. According to the article in the *North County Times*, similar displays also occurred at The Citadel in Los Angeles and at several malls owned by Craig Realty of Texas.

"This location is great," said retired police officer Michael Woods, who works with NCMEC, talking about the Lake Elsinore sign. "This is a major thoroughfare [Interstate 15] for lots of trucks. Truckers are very valuable because they traverse the entire country, and they communicate within the trucking community."[31] Reflecting on what Officer Woods said, parents of long-term runaways should definitely attempt to post their missing child fliers, with an age-progression picture on them, at every truck stop they can.

Another spot the parents of long-term runaway children should attempt to post their fliers at is Interstate rest stops. Runaways will often try to hitchhike a ride at these rest stops with truckers and others. Some other possibilities for missing child flier distribution include large retail centers, inside business mailings, national meetings of organizations in the area, pizza delivery personnel, and package delivery services. The many sources of distribution for missing child fliers are limited only to the parents' imagination.

5. Parents of long-term runaway children should post any videos of their children on the YouTube Missing Children's Channel at www. youtube.com/DontYouForgetAbout Me.

6. If they haven't done it already, parents of long-term runaway children should list their missing children with NCMEC at 1-800-843-5678 or www.missingkids.com. Since 1984, NCMEC has assisted law enforcement with more than 160,000 missing children cases, resulting in the recovery of more than 145,000 missing children.[32] Also, NCMEC can help distribute missing child fliers. This organization has access to over 26,000 places to send these fliers, including police departments, missing children clearinghouses, the Border Patrol,

medical examiner offices, and others. Parents should also request that NCMEC do an age-progression picture of their child to put on the flier. Children can change considerably in the months or years they are gone. But more important for the parents of a long-term runaway child, NCMEC has a Cold Case Unit that looks for children who have been missing for a long time. In the Winter 2007 issue of *Frontline*, the newsletter of NCMEC, an article tells about the success of this unit, which has recovered twelve long-term missing children alive and identified the remains of 327 missing children who have died. In 2007, they reported having 200 open cases they were working on.

7. Parents should contact the various runaway hotlines with information about their children. These include the National Runaway Switchboard at 1-800-RUNAWAY, Child Find of America at 1-800-I-AM-LOST, the National Missing Children's Locate Center at 1-800-999-7846, Covenant House at 1-800-999-9999, and the California Youth Crisis Line at 1-800-843-5200. Also, parents need to put their children's information on websites such as the North American Missing Persons Network at www.nampn.org, Help Find the Missing at www.helpfindthemissing.org, and the National Missing and Unidentified Persons System at www.findthemissing.org. In addition, the parents of long-term runaways should contact the DOE Network at 931-397-3893 or at www.doenetwork.org and put their children's information on this site. The DOE Network is an organization set up specifically for long-term missing persons. Finally, parents should also contact the Runaway Assistance Program at 1-877-4-A-RUNAWAY or at http://runawaysquad.com/rap/.

8. According to the web-based Encyclopedia of Children's Health, there are over 750 runaway shelters and youth crisis centers in the United States.[33] Parents of long-term runaways need to get on the Internet and send each one of these sites a copy of their missing child poster. If children have been missing for a long time there is a good chance that they have stopped in at one of these locations for help. Since these centers are often very protective of the children they serve, parents should be certain to include a message of care and love either with the flier or on it. In some states the law requires that anyone who gives shelter to a runaway must report the runaway to the police. Therefore, sending a

missing child poster to every runaway shelter could result in one of them being forced to report the child to the local police.

"I think a lot of youth service agencies are kind of going right now on sort of a 'don't ask, don't tell' policy," said Rachel Meyers of Covenant House. "If you don't ask a kid if they ran away and their parent doesn't want them to be gone, then you have a reason to think that maybe it's okay for them to be away from home."[34] This type of reasoning is why parents must send a missing child flier to every runaway shelter in America. That way there is no question that the children are away from home without permission.

Also, while I have mentioned a number of missing children organizations in this chapter, there are many more. Parents need to get on the Internet and send every one they can find a copy of their missing child poster. Parents never know where their children may have turned to for help.

9. As we have talked about, a missing child poster must include information on it that lets runaway children know they are more than welcome to return home. Children who have been gone for long periods of time will often believe that no one cares or is looking for them any longer. A poster should make the children realize that people do care and are still looking for them.

10. Parents of long-term runaway children should contact their state missing children clearinghouse to be certain their children are listed there. Although the police should have listed a runaway child there, they may not have, so parents should make certain they did. While there, parents should also investigate what resources these organizations have available to assist them. The addresses of all state missing children clearinghouses can be found in the appendix of *When Your Child Is Missing: A Family Survival Guide*.

11. The Missing Children Investigation Agency is a nonprofit organization that can assist parents in the search for their runaway children. This agency works with volunteers from law enforcement and other areas to search for missing and runaway children. They can be reached at www.kidfind.org or at 1-818-382-1999.

12. Another organization the parents of long-term runaway children should contact is the Association of Missing and Exploited

Children's Organizations, Inc. at www.amecoinc.org or at 1-877-263-2620. This group can give parents the names of the various nonprofit missing children organizations in their area.

13. Parents of long-term runaway children might want to consider offering a reward for information about their children's location. However, as I advised above, parents should be sure to seek legal advice first as this can become a legally binding contract.

14. An option that won't be cheap, but that can often be very effective, is the hiring of a private investigator. Some of these individuals have had great success in finding runaways. Also, private investigators, unlike police departments, don't have to worry about jurisdictional lines or following certain restrictive rules and policies. In addition, unlike police departments, private investigators don't have hundreds and sometimes thousands of competing cases. As the website for one such detective agency, ICS, said, "Working with ICS as well as the police department has other advantages. For example, ICS is not hampered by crossing jurisdictional lines or having to deal with any internal police politics. ICS does not have to deal with some of the flack that some police departments encounter that might slow an investigation down. We can save valuable time in a missing child investigation."[35]

A number of sources pointed out that the case of Brandi Stahr, discussed in chapter 1, could have been solved much quicker by a private investigator. While police officers are handcuffed by restrictions against accessing certain information on people, private investigators have no such restrictions. However, before parents hire a private investigator they need to be certain that he or she is experienced in this field, and also demand and check references.

I had an interesting conversation recently at a social gathering of present and former homicide detectives. I was talking with a retired police officer who is now a private investigator. I told him about the book I was writing on finding missing persons, and he told me about how he had recently found a person who had disappeared years before. I asked him how he did it, and he told me, "I can't tell you," meaning that he had used some means that likely would have gotten him into trouble if he had still been a police officer.

Debra Gwartney, mentioned above, who had two long-term runaway daughters, decided to hire a private detective. "I hired a private investigator, finally, to search for them," she said. "He was a former Los Angeles cop, and he had a reputation of being able to find kids pretty quickly. He found them within 24 hours."[36]

"It's always going to be a benefit to have an experienced PI on any case," Ed Opperman of Opperman Investigations out of Las Vegas told me. "Not to interfere with or compete with a police investigation, but to gather facts and put it together in a neat report to present to his client and the police. Let's face it, a PI has a financial incentive to keep his clients happy by producing good results. He's going to work hard for his clients in the hope of getting future work or referrals out of the case."[37]

15. Cults regularly take in runaway children. Parents of long-term runaways should check with any cult awareness centers in their area.

16. Strip clubs often use older runaway females as strippers. This is why, as I advised, it could be helpful for the parents of long-term runaways to send information about the runaways to the local vice squads.

17. Parents of long-term runaway children should obtain from NCMEC the booklet: "A Child Is Missing: Providing Support for Families of Missing Children." This booklet can help parents cope emotionally and psychologically with their child's disappearance. Also, Team Hope at www.teamhope.org is a group of parents who have experienced the pain of a missing child. They can be great for support and assistance during the search for a runaway child.

18. Finally, a possibility parents must consider after enough time passes without any word from or about their runaway children is that they might be deceased. As we talked about in chapter 4, approximately 5,000 runaway and homeless children die every year. Parents of long-term runaway children, therefore, should contact the medical examiner or coroner's offices in their area. If parents have fingerprints, medical records, dental charts, or DNA, these can be very useful in identifying any unclaimed bodies. If necessary, DNA for a runaway child can be recovered from a hairbrush or toothbrush. Also, parents need to log on to http://identifyus.org to see if any of the unidentified remains on this

site might be their child. As of November 2010, this site had 7,044 open cases of unidentified remains.

In addition, parents should check in with www.namus.gov. This is the National Missing and Unidentified Persons System. This site has access to over 40,000 sets of unidentified remains sitting in medical examiner and coroner's offices across the United States. This system, which went online in 2009, almost immediately identified the remains of a sixteen-year-old runaway boy, who had been missing for fourteen years. This site will list what identifiers are available on the remains, and if parents believe there may be a match, a DNA comparison can be done. More information about this site will be included in chapter 8.

Of course, as everyone knows, it is not only juveniles who run away or simply disappear. Every year, many thousands of adults also vanish. As we will see in the next chapter, like juveniles, adults can have many reasons for wanting to disappear.

· 6 ·

Why Do Adults Disappear?

$\mathcal{I}$n March 2006, eighteen-year-old Laura Mackenzie's family was beset by turmoil. Laura's grandmother had died recently and her brother had just been deployed to Iraq. On March 8, 2006, the turmoil for the Goffstown, New Hampshire, family became even worse when Laura suddenly disappeared. Laura, an honor student who excelled at track, simply vanished that day and no one, including her boyfriend, saw anything in her behavior that could have foretold this. Consequently, no one knew if she had left voluntarily or perhaps had been abducted.

At around 9:00 AM on March 8, Laura told her family that she had to take her 1995 Volkswagen for an oil change. No one saw her after that. What her family didn't know was that on March 8 Laura also had a date in court to answer felony shoplifting charges, a situation she had kept secret from everyone.

Laura's family, naturally distraught at her disappearance, notified the police, and then began posting missing person fliers all around town. They simply couldn't believe that she would just leave. And even after eventually finding out about the pending criminal charges, her family still didn't think that Laura would just abandon her home and family over this. Instead, they feared that she might have been the victim of foul play, particularly since she had very little financial resources when she disappeared.

"We just hope she's safe and that no one is keeping her against her will and that she's able to call home," said Enid Mackenzie, Laura's mother.[1]

The police, on the other hand, weren't totally convinced that Laura was a victim of foul play, but didn't totally rule it out either. "Right now, we're looking at it as a conscious effort by the young lady to leave," said Captain Glenn Dubois of the Goffstown Police Department. But then he added, "We haven't ruled anything out."[2]

On April 7, 2006, Goffstown hosted a candlelight vigil for the missing girl, those attending the ceremony joining in a prayer for Laura's safe return. Her family, now desperate for any news about Laura, offered a $5,000 reward for information leading to her safe return. Even the FBI became involved in the search for Laura.

Fortunately, Laura's family, never giving up hope, managed to have her story included in a Public Service Announcement that followed the popular CBS television show *Without a Trace*, a program that depicts a fictional account of the FBI's Missing Persons Unit. This proved to be the impetus needed to locate Laura.

On August 7, 2006, a man who saw the Public Service Announcement recognized Laura as a woman who worked as a waitress in a beachfront restaurant in St. Augustine Beach, Florida. The Hillsborough County (New Hampshire) Sheriff's Department, upon receiving this information, notified the police in St. Augustine Beach, who, after checking at the restaurant, went to an apartment building where Laura lived. There, they found Laura and arrested her on the outstanding shoplifting charge. They also found her Volkswagen, with the New Hampshire plates still on it, parked nearby. Laura later said that to avoid detection she had not used her bank card or checked her e-mail and had driven her car as little as possible.

In September 2006, on a website started in an effort to locate another missing teen, Laura issued an apology. "I am sorry, and I need to ask everyone to forgive me for what I did, putting them through the hardships and pain of 5 long months where I was missing."[3]

Laura Mackenzie obviously felt that she had a very good reason for disappearing. She had kept her arrest for shoplifting a secret from everyone. However, on March 8, 2006, when she was scheduled to appear in court, Laura knew that her secret would soon be revealed to her family, her friends, and to everyone in the small community where she lived. For the never-in-trouble honor student, it was simply too much to face.

Pending criminal charges or the possibility that a person will be exposed as being involved in criminal activity is a popular reason for adults to disappear. In the following incident, the authorities believe that involvement in criminal activity and the likelihood of its imminent exposure led to the sudden disappearance of a Grahmn, Washington man.

Fifty-one-year-old Darrel Kempf had operated Triad Marketing, a used car dealership in rural Washington, for over eleven years. His company purchased vehicles at car auctions and then resold them. He also took in cars and sold them on consignment. For most people who knew Kempf he seemed to be a very congenial and honest person to deal with.

"Extremely personable," said Jason Kath, one of Kempf's customers, "someone that I would do business with again, extremely trustworthy."[4]

However, rather than personable and trustworthy, Kempf was allegedly a conman, who perpetrated a number of frauds on unsuspecting victims. In one of these, he took money from individuals for vehicles he was selling on consignment and then pocketed the money rather than passing it on to the people who held the car titles. In another, he took out fraudulent car loans.

"I believe we're probably talking about three million dollars right now," said one of Kempf's victims, Greg Krueger, who had loaned money to Kempf through Automotive Finance Corporation.[5]

In January 2007, the police, for some time suspicious of Kempf and his activities, were beginning to close in on him. However, Kempf apparently realized this.

On January 28, 2007, the police found a car believed to be operated by Kempf overturned off a cliff along a remote stretch of a Pacific coast highway. Rather than finding a body inside the car, however, the officers instead found that the steering wheel had been secured with a belt. They could find no indication that anyone had been in the car when it left the road. The police investigation consequently ruled it a staged scene. They believe Kempf likely thought that the car would explode and burn when it hit the bottom of the cliff, leading the authorities to believe that he had died in the crash.

A police dog located a scent trail for Kempf on the highway close to where his vehicle had left the road. It ran for a short distance and then stopped, meaning that Kempf had likely gotten into another vehicle. There has been no sign of Kempf since then. Fourteen felony charges for theft and forgery have since been issued for Kempf, and the Washington police have notified the authorities in all other states to be on the lookout for him.

Of course, the various criminal acts that people disappear because of aren't limited to only theft and forgery as in the above incidents. Sometimes it is something much more serious, such as sexual assault, child molestation, or other violent crimes. In these cases, the person disappearing is not only worried about public shame, but also about the possibility of a lengthy prison term.

Along with criminal activity as a reason to disappear, adults can also vanish because they are reluctant witnesses in someone else's criminal or civil trial. These individuals know that they will be forced to appear in court and testify under oath, but don't want to for various reasons: because it may reflect badly on them, because the person they're testifying against is a friend, or because they fear that the person they're testifying against will retaliate.

Also on the subject of criminal activity and the courts, readers should keep in mind that an adult might seem to disappear, but not actually be missing. Some missing individuals may have simply been sentenced to jail or prison and not want anyone to know about it.

In addition to criminal activity, there are also many other reasons adults may choose to disappear. For example, individuals may find themselves so far in debt, with a dozen credit cards maxed out and mortgage payments six months behind, that the only way they can see to get themselves out of these desperate straits is by disappearing and then starting all over again somewhere else as a different person. This, of course, isn't an easy thing to do, since these individuals usually leave with very limited financial resources, and consequently they soon find themselves in serious financial difficulties again.

In addition to huge credit card bills and other debts, some individuals will disappear in order to escape having to make alimony or child support payments. Other individuals, because they feel responsible for getting their families so far into debt, want desperately to rescue their families, and they do this by faking their deaths and then disappearing, hoping their families can cash in on their life insurance policies. For others, though, as in the incident below, personal excesses can lead to so much debt that the person feels that fleeing is the only option.

Thomas Gregory Demyon, forty-seven, was the vice-president of Safety/Sight Inc. of Cockeysville, Maryland, when he suddenly disappeared on January 13, 1997. Thomas told his wife that he had received an emergency page from his attorney, but since the telephone service had been turned off where he and his wife were staying he needed to drive to the nearby Days Inn to use their pay phone. He never returned, and his attorney later said that he never made any emergency call to Thomas. His wife reported his disappearance to the police, who, upon their investigation, didn't believe foul play was involved. Thomas, as it turned out, had been a serious gambler who had often visited Las Vegas and Atlantic City. Reportedly, the police found, he was heavily in debt to a number of people because of his gambling.

For some adults, family responsibilities can occasionally become just too much for them to bear, and so they disappear. The arrival of a new baby with several children at home already, aging parents that need constant care, rebellious teenagers, children always in some kind of trouble, and other family stressors can make some individuals feel that disappearing is the only way they will ever have a peaceful life. In addition, constant conflict with in-laws or domestic violence between married partners can also be the push behind a person's sudden disappearance.

Along with family problems, sometimes the occupation a person chooses can become so stressful that the individual may want to flee.

Some jobs, even though paying well, can expect a total commitment that many people aren't willing to make.

Of course, in addition to all of the above, some individuals may have pictured their lives much different than they turned out. High expectations can often run into brutal reality, and some people may feel that if they stay in their present situation, nothing is ever going to change and they will never realize their dreams. So they disappear.

Another reason for adults to suddenly become missing is because they have joined a cult. People who join cults can vanish without a clue as to what happened to them. As I talk about in my book *Deadly Cults: The Crimes of True Believers*, many cults insist on total isolation from the outside world for its members. Any contact with individuals from their life prior to joining the cult is considered contamination and strictly forbidden. Also, some cults will send new recruits to sites far away from their home so that they will have no source of support other than the cult.

Along with everything we've talked about so far, another variable to consider when an adult suddenly and inexplicably disappears is the person's medical or mental condition. As the following incident illustrates, a failure to take medicine can often be the cause of a missing person incident.

The family of twenty-two-year-old Joshua Stefanski became alarmed when he suddenly disappeared from his Kent County, Michigan, home in November 2010. Joshua has a medical condition in which he becomes confused and disoriented if he doesn't take his medicine. The authorities were particularly concerned in this case because wandering around in the cold November air of Michigan can quickly lead to hypothermia. Consequently, the police launched an immediate search for the young man. The authorities used boats to search the Rogue River near Joshua's home, and they also utilized helicopters with night vision technology. Along with this, the police brought in a K-9 tracking team.

Fortunately, members of the Grand Rapids Police Department, notified of the disappearance, found Joshua wandering the streets of Grand Rapids, miles from his home. Although confused, Joshua appeared to be in good physical condition.

"It's our understanding that he walked a portion of the way and then rode a city bus into the downtown area and then was just randomly walking around downtown Grand Rapids since yesterday, and it's also possible that he slept underneath the freeway last night," said Sergeant Tom Raymond of the Kent County Sheriff's Department.[6]

A possibility that the families of missing individuals naturally don't want to think about, but still must consider, is that someone may be missing because he or she has committed or wants to commit suicide. Suicidal individuals often don't want to do it where someone might come along and stop them or where family members would find the body. Also, some individuals will disappear to commit suicide with the hope that family members will never know what happened to them. As the following incidents show, this can happen with individuals few would expect to be suicidal.

When fifty-nine-year-old Robert Hughes left his home in Williamsville, Vermont, on August 17, 2008, he told his family that he had to go to a business meeting in Provincetown, Massachusetts. He never showed up. Three days later, his wife received an envelope in the mail from him. In it were letters to his family that stated he planned to kill himself in the White Mountains of New Hampshire. He also told family members where his car could be found, which the police later recovered. To date, his body is yet to be located.

In another case, on May 23, 2010, fifty-four-year-old Debra Rixey of Fairfield, California, visited a friend, but then never returned home. Her family, extremely concerned for her welfare, reported her as missing to the police. The authorities soon found her 2001 Honda Civic abandoned in a secluded area of Nevada County, California. In the trunk, officers found Debra's body. At first, the police believed this to be a homicide, but soon realized it wasn't.

"Apparently she left notes to family members and it looks like she consumed a large quantity of prescription drugs," said Nevada County Sheriff Keith Royal. "It looks like it was an intentional overdose."[7]

Finally, Brad Collier, fifty-three, had a long and distinguished career in law enforcement. He began as a Hillsdale, New Jersey, police officer and then joined the Drug Enforcement Administration (DEA), where he served as a special agent. After retiring from federal service in the DEA, Collier served for almost two years as the director of the Edison Township (New Jersey) Police Department, a department that, because of Collier's reputation in law enforcement, he was hired to clean up.

On February 26, 2010, his family notified the police that Collier was missing. Searchers eventually located his body in a secluded section of Wood Dale County Park. The medical examiner ruled Collier's death a suicide. He reportedly had been struggling to cope with the sudden death of his twenty-year-old daughter. Collier had been married with three other children.

"The man was very dedicated," said Edison Police Chief Thomas Bryan. "But not only that, he was a caring guy. He was a tremendous person."[8]

While we have covered in this chapter a number of the major reasons adults will suddenly go missing, there are many people who disappear for reasons that no one will ever know. Often, people can be very private and will hide their true feelings from even those close to them. These individuals, while outwardly appearing happy, can actually be extremely unhappy with their lives and one day just decide to leave and start over somewhere else. Readers will remember that in chapter 1 we talked about a woman who disappeared with food still cooking on the stove. When located some time later she said that she just wanted a change in her life. This behavior is much more common than most people would suspect. Ohio Intel, a detective agency that specializes in finding missing persons, said on their website, "Based on our experiences, family members are not always aware of the actual circumstances surrounding a person's disappearance and are often surprised upon discovery of the facts."[9]

In this chapter we have talked exclusively about the reasons adults disappear voluntarily. However, as we will see in the next chapter, occasionally adults also go missing for reasons beyond their control. These individuals can disappear because they are the victims of a crime or an accident.

· 7 ·

Missing Adult:
Crime Victim or Accident Victim?

$\mathcal{S}$heldon Scott, a legally blind sixty-seven-year-old man, lived with his wife in a ten-story apartment building in the Riverdale area of the Bronx in New York City. Although handicapped by his lack of sight, that didn't stop Sheldon from getting out and around in the neighborhood.

"He trusted me to help him, to handle his money," said Genevieve Martinez, a worker at a delicatessen near where Sheldon lived. "He became like a father type."[1]

So when, on April 30, 2009, Sheldon didn't return home when he should have his wife Eileen naturally became concerned. She knew he had gone to the bank and should have returned within the hour. Eileen called 911 and reported him as missing. Because of Sheldon's handicap, officers began an immediate search of the area, but found no sign of him.

The next day, however, the police found Sheldon's body at the bottom of an elevator shaft in the apartment building where he and his wife had lived since 1954. Apparently, the elevators in the building were being worked on, and the authorities theorize that the door must have opened onto an empty shaft. Because of his lack of sight, Sheldon stepped in and fell to his death.

"This is very unfortunate, but if he wasn't blind this probably wouldn't have happened," said Scott T. Hayes, an elevator consultant. "But even sighted people can fall down a shaft if they are not paying attention."[2]

The police in Portland, Oregon, responded to a missing person report on January 17, 2010. Neighbors told the police that they had spoken with fifty-seven-year-old Michael Zerwas on January 14, but that he hadn't been seen since. The neighbors said that on that day Michael had complained to them about water mysteriously bubbling up in his yard. Police officers searched Michael's home, but found no clues as to the reason for his disappearance and no signs of foul play. In his backyard, however, officers discovered a pair of muddy crocs-style shoes next to a watery hole almost hidden by shrubbery. The hole appeared to be either an old well or cesspool. The police called for the fire department to come and pump the water out of what turned out to be a twenty-five-foot-deep abandoned cesspool that had been boarded over when the city hooked the house up to sewers in 1977.

After the fire department had emptied the water from the cesspool, the police found Michael's body. An autopsy showed that he had died of hypothermia and eventual drowning. The police believe that the cesspool cover caved in under Michael's feet as he was investigating the water bubbling up in his yard.

In the above two incidents, individuals reported to the police as missing hadn't disappeared voluntarily. Instead, they had been the victims of unfortunate accidents. And while the police located these two victims within a day or two of their reported disappearance, that isn't always the case. Sometimes, as in the following incidents, it can be years before family and friends find out that a missing person actually died in an accident rather than running off to seek a new life.

A person skin diving in the Gallants Channel offshore of Beaufort, North Carolina, in October 2009, discovered a 1998 Jeep Cherokee submerged in the water. Upon learning of this, the local sheriff's department sent a dive team to the area and, with the use of underwater sonar, they located the vehicle. The deputies then had the Jeep pulled from the water and transported to a secure site for forensic examination.

The authorities found the body of twenty-six-year-old George Edward Quinn still strapped inside the vehicle. Quinn had last been heard from over four and a half years earlier when he made a telephone call to his girlfriend from a Beaufort-area telephone. Soon afterward, his family had reported him as missing, and while the police at the time searched for Quinn, they could find no sign of him.

In a similar case, in November 2010, the police in Jacksonville, Florida, responded to the report of a citizen finding a vehicle submerged in the lake in front of Mandarin High School. The police had the vehicle, a 1993 turquoise Saturn, pulled from the water. Inside, they discovered the body of Francis Watson, who had been reported missing from his home in Lake City, Florida, on March 3, 2006.

Of course, missing people such as these don't always turn up dead. If for some reason they are injured and unconscious but not carrying any identification, they can be sent to a hospital, but then no one is notified because the missing people can't identify themselves. Or, as in the following incident, they may be so mentally incapacitated that they can't tell workers at the hospital who they are.

The Riverside, California, police released thirty-nine-year-old Noemi Venegas from jail soon after her arrest in November 2010 for involvement in a family disturbance. Before family members could get to the jail to pick her up though, she had disappeared. Because Noemi suffers from a mental condition that can cause confusion and disorientation, her family became concerned and reported her to the authorities as missing.

In their attempt to find her, Noemi's family had missing person fliers printed up. For five days, they waited to hear news about Noemi, but none came and family members began to fear the worst. Finally though, the family received some very good news. Noemi had been in the hospital for the last five days, but the family didn't know it.

Of course, sometimes foul play, rather than accident, is the cause of a person's disappearance. Often, a murderer doesn't want the body found and tries to hide it. Consequently, the family members of the victim usually don't know what's going on, and so they report the loved one's disappearance to the police. As the following incidents demonstrate, sometimes the body of a missing person who has fallen victim to foul play is discovered soon after the murder, but in some cases it can be years before family members learn the fate of their missing loved one.

Twenty-six-year-old Alex Casillas had been the boyfriend of thirty-year-old Yesenia Lilly for a long time and had lived with her in an apartment in Brentwood, Long Island, New York, for two years. When Yesenia and her eleven-year-old son James suddenly disappeared, Alex filed a missing person report with the police.

Along with family members, Alex helped pass out missing person fliers. He even cried with the family as they sat and worried about what could have happened to Yesenia and James.

However, the police became suspicious of Alex because of conflicting stories he told about the last time he had seen Yesenia, and they were particularly suspicious because of Alex's past record. When he and Yesenia met, Alex had just been released from prison, where he had served four years for reportedly sexually assaulting a woman. Yesenia and her family knew about Alex's past, but felt that he had changed and was now a good man.

Upon questioning by the police, Alex's story began to fall apart, and he finally broke down and confessed that after Yesenia had confronted him about an affair she suspected him of having, he had slashed her throat, dismembered her, and then stuffed her remains into a trash bag. He also confessed to strangling James to death because he had witnessed the murder. After his confession, Alex led the police to a wooded area behind a factory where he had once worked and showed them where he had dumped the bodies.

"I want him to rot in jail," said Yesenia's sister Liz. "He cried with us."[3]

In another incident, forty-six-year-old Eridania Rodriquez punched in for work as a cleaning lady at a twenty-six-story building near Ground Zero in New York City. This was at 5:00 PM on July 7, 2009. Security cameras last recorded seeing her in the building at around 7:00 PM. Following this, she disappeared. Security cameras didn't record her leaving the building.

Police officers investigating her disappearance found Eridania's street clothes and purse still in her locker. They also discovered her cleaning cart abandoned on the eighth floor. Investigators searched the entire building but didn't come up with a single clue as to what had happened to Eridania.

"It's a mind blower," said Rob Ross, a tenant of the building. "How do you go missing here?"[4]

Four days later, the body of Eridania finally turned up. She had been bound and gagged, and stuffed into an air duct in the building. The autopsy showed the cause of death to be asphyxiation.

The case immediately changed from that of a missing person to a homicide. "She had been complaining about a guy in the building who made her kind of nervous," said Daniel Ferreira, a lawyer for Eridania's family.[5]

DNA from skin found under Eridania's fingernails eventually led the police to twenty-five-year-old Joseph Pabon, an elevator operator in the building. They arrested him and charged him with Eridania's murder. Police said that Pabon had bruises on his biceps and sides, along with scratches on his neck and hands.

In a case in which the victim was not found as quickly as in the two above, twenty-three-year-old Darlene Campos disappeared in April 2001 after attending a family Easter celebration in Lakewood, Washington. A year later, hikers found the decomposed body of a woman in a creek in Peasley Canyon, near Auburn, Washington, about twenty-five miles northeast of Lakewood. The police, however, couldn't immediately identify the remains.

The authorities had a forensic artist develop a sketch of what the woman would have looked like and also had the manufacturer of the jeans found on the body make a new pair so that pictures of the jeans could be circulated with the artist's likeness. However, neither of these produced any results.

Then, three years following the discovery of the body, Dr. Kathy Taylor, a forensic anthropologist for the King County (Washington) Medical Examiner's Office, visited the website of the North American Missing Persons Network. While there, she found information about Darlene.

"I looked at her bio and she fit perfectly," said Dr. Taylor. "As soon as her picture popped up, I knew it was her."[6]

The police, once the body had been identified, began investigating Darlene's case as a murder investigation rather than a missing person. They arrested Darlene's boyfriend, who eventually admitted to strangling her during an argument.

Finally, a missing person case that took thirty years to solve occurred on Long Island, New York in 1999. There, the police found a steel drum buried under a house. Inside the drum they discovered the mummified remains of a pregnant woman named Reyna Marroquin. The authorities identified her through a document in the barrel that contained her Social Security number. Reyna had been reported missing in 1969. The owner of the house, Howard Elkin, who also owned the flower business where Reyna worked, killed himself when confronted by the police about the barrel.

In all of the incidents we have talked about in this chapter the missing person, who was actually the victim of an accident or murder, was located and the case closed. Readers should keep in mind that in many unsolved missing person cases the individual may still have been the victim of an accident or murder, but just never found. No one knows how many missing persons are really not voluntarily missing at all, but dead from an accident or murder. The number likely is very large.

The main point I am making in this chapter is that people shouldn't immediately blame themselves or torture themselves with questions about what they did that made their loved one so unhappy that he or she left. As we have seen in this chapter, sometimes the disappearance is not a matter of someone running away. The Los Angeles Police Department, for example, reports that 15 percent of their missing person cases are nonvoluntary.[7]

In the next chapter we are going to talk about the people who, rather than the victims of accidents or murders, really are voluntarily missing. I will show readers how, with just a bit of effort and perseverance, they can find these people.

Finding Missing Adults

𝒥ackie Rains-Kracman, a nineteen-year-old mother of two, lived in Columbus, Nebraska. Melvin Uphoff, a thirty-year-old father of four, lived in nearby Rising City, Nebraska. Both worked at the Rising City Co-op. It was September 1965, and the rumor around the area was that the two were having an affair. In support of this rumor, Jackie's husband had recently filed for divorce.

On September 24, 1965, Jackie told her family that she would be gone for a few days. She said she was going to attend a girlfriend's wedding in Glenwood, Iowa, a town a little over a hundred miles to the east-south-east.

Jackie's sister, Sharon Henggeler, remembered it being odd that Jackie packed so much clothing for such a short trip. "She was packing everything," said Sharon. "I asked her 'Why?' She said she needed to put these clothes somewhere."[1]

Even with all of the clothing she took, no one in her family worried about Jackie leaving town. They didn't believe there was even the slightest chance she wouldn't return, that she would abandon her children. But she didn't return home, and her family was stunned when they checked and found that there had been no wedding in Iowa. Jackie had simply disappeared.

On October 24, 1965, Melvin and his family had spent the day in nearby Shelby, Nebraska. He and his wife took their four children roller skating, went out to eat, and stayed at a hotel. When they returned home to Rising City, Melvin told his wife that he was going out for a beer and would return soon. He drove away in his 1954 blue and white Oldsmobile, and his wife never saw him again. He took no clothing. The only thing his wife could find missing was his prized coin collection.

The local sheriff at the time, Leo Mesiter, investigated the disappearance of the two people and concluded that they had run away to be together. He didn't find any evidence of foul play.

Family members of the couple didn't agree. No one, they insisted, would just run off and abandon six children that both Jackie and Melvin seemed to adore. The families instead felt certain that Jackie and Melvin had been the victims of some heinous crime, and continued to pressure the sheriff to find out what had really happened to them. The sheriff, though, just couldn't buy into the theory of foul play.

"It haunts me," Sheriff Meister said of the case. "I want to find Mr. Uphoff and walk him right down Main Street in Rising City and let everyone know he's alive."[2]

It would take over forty years, however, before anyone would find out what had really happened to Jackie and Melvin. In 2009, the Nebraska State Patrol, which had been working on the case for several years, marked it as solved and closed. They had received a tip and then located the couple, now ages seventy-four and sixty-three, doing well and living in another state. Sheriff Meister had been right all along.

According to a news account of the case, "The couple today tells the State Patrol, they want to be left alone and want privacy."[3]

Denise Bolser, a twenty-four-year-old bookkeeper who lived in Raymond, New Hampshire, suddenly disappeared in January 1985. Inside the home she and her husband shared, the husband found a note that said, "We've got your wife."

Several days later, the police discovered a pickup truck belonging to the Bolsers parked at Logan Airport in Boston. On the front seat officers found Denise's Social Security card, birth certificate, and local charge cards.

The police never did classify Denise's disappearance as a kidnapping, but rather believed that she had left voluntarily. Her parents, however, whom Denise had reportedly been very close to, simply could not accept that she would just up and leave and never contact them again. They instead felt convinced that she had been the victim of foul play. Denise's husband, however, apparently not sharing the same feeling, divorced her after she disappeared.

For seventeen years the case remained an open missing person investigation. New Hampshire State Trooper Roland Lamy had gone to school with Denise's parents, and so he took the case personally and kept it alive. He knew that Denise's disappearance was causing her parents terrible anguish, particularly with them not knowing whether their daughter was alive or dead.

"These are good, solid people from the West Side of Manchester and they suffered greatly," said Trooper Lamy. "I never once thought she was dead."[4]

Trooper Lamy persuaded Lieutenant Shawne Coope of the Raymond, New Hampshire Police Department to become involved in investigating the case with him. The two detectives did all they could to keep the case alive in the print and visual media. They also made sure to have the case listed on numerous Internet missing-person sites.

Finally, in 2002, a private detective in Florida named Shirley Casey, who specializes in finding missing persons, was looking at a missing person website, the DOE Network. Denise's case looked interesting to her because Casey's family had come from New Hampshire. The website said that if Denise was alive she would be living in a warm climate. Casey then began looking up the name Denise in Florida databases and came up with one that had the same birth date as Denise Bolser: June 1, 1960. She passed this information along to the police in Raymond, New Hampshire.

"I just passed the information along," said Casey. "It sounded like it was their gal."[5]

On May 13, 2002, police officers knocked on a door in Panama City, Florida, where a woman calling herself Denise James reportedly lived. Denise Bolser, who had since remarried, opened the door, knew her secret was out, and broke down crying. Denise's new husband, who knew nothing about his wife's previous life, said that finding out the truth answered a lot of questions for him.

"It was such a good feeling," said David Salois, retired Raymond police chief. "To get closure on a case like this and to find her alive. Her family never gave up hope and we finally had the best news for them."[6]

What these two cases have in common, besides the fact that three missing people who had been gone for a very long time were located, is that none of these people wanted to be found. We touched on this a bit in chapter 1, but the point I'm trying to make here is that individuals searching for missing people who have left voluntarily should realize that this endeavor can sometimes be a long, tedious, often frustrating, and many times expensive undertaking. And, even if completed successfully, the endeavor will not bring about a happy reunion if the missing people don't want to be found. Therefore, individuals seeking someone who has disappeared voluntarily should realize before they start that often years of work, while perhaps providing a sense of closure in the knowledge that their loved one is still alive, may nevertheless leave them disheartened if upon being found the person does not want to renew old relationships.

"When the reasons are clear and reasonable, such as trying to alert someone that the head of a family is in ill health or has died—or better yet—has left the person a legacy in his or her will, it's a pleasure to take on these jobs," private investigator Leigh Hearon told me. "Even so, I caution clients that if I'm successful in tracking down the person, I will first make contact and give the 'found' person the option to pass on his or her contact information. People disappear for all kinds of reasons, and simply because I find them doesn't mean that I have the right to invade their privacy without their approval."[7]

How many missing adults leave home voluntarily like this? The Los Angeles Police Department reports that it takes almost 4,000 missing adult reports every year, and that "85 percent of missing person cases are so-called 'voluntaries,' individuals who are missing by design and want to stay lost."[8]

Of course, it may also be that the person left for reasons other than because he or she wanted to separate totally from the old life and everyone in it, and these individuals may welcome renewed contact. But, in the end, searchers may not care if the missing person wants to renew relationships; they simply want to be certain the missing person is alive and well. Often parents and loved ones of a missing person live in anguish for many years, torturing themselves over the question of whether or not the missing person is safe, healthy, or even alive. An article, for example, in the *Seattle Times* tells of the case of a mother who wouldn't leave her apartment for a year because she was certain her missing daughter would call, and she was afraid that she would miss the call if she wasn't there.[9] And finally, many individuals searching for missing people may anticipate a cold reception, but are willing to risk it because they simply want answers about why the person left. For these people there are many things searchers can do to locate a missing adult.

The first thing to do in a missing adult case, unless there is obvious evidence of foul play or imminent danger to the person, is to check with family, friends, and coworkers to be certain the person isn't missing simply because of a misunderstanding about where he or she was supposed to be. Also, check to be certain that the missing person hasn't left a message or note, including on the computer, explaining where he or she is at. In addition, searchers should call all local hospitals. This shouldn't take long, and if it doesn't turn up the person, loved ones should then call the police and report the person as missing.

The website of the Phoenix Police Department has some advice on when to call the police for missing adults: "First contact all family and friends of the missing person to ensure there was not a miscommunication, traffic delay, or other reason for their disappearance. Make every attempt to contact and locate the missing person before filing a report."[10]

However, as I cautioned above, if foul play or imminent danger, including the possibility of suicide, is present, loved ones shouldn't wait, but call the police right away. Also, if a person goes missing in a rugged, sparsely populated area, it is extremely important to report the disappearance immediately. A study of 4,244 search and rescue missions carried out in Oregon, where individuals will often go missing in wilderness areas, discovered that 99 percent of the people found alive were found within fifty-one hours.[11]

In most cases of missing adults, the police will take a report and, if the conditions discussed in chapter 1 are present, they will enter the missing adult's information into the FBI's National Crime Information Center (NCIC) computer system. An important measure to take in the case of a missing adult who is believed to be the victim of foul play or who is endangered for some other reason is for family members to submit a copy of the missing person's DNA to the police. This DNA can come from a personal item the missing person may have used, such as a hairbrush or toothbrush. Also, comparison samples from close family members may be needed. These can be taken by simply running a cotton swab inside the cheek. The police can then have these DNA samples entered into the FBI's Combined DNA Index System (CODIS) and afterward uploaded into the NCIC's Missing Person DNA Database. What is the value of this? In the event unidentified human remains turn up somewhere, the police can verify the person's identity if his or her DNA is on file. In December 2010, for example, the police used DNA to close the case of the remains of a missing person discovered in Louisiana in 1979.[12] The power of DNA for the identification of human remains is tremendous.

Investigators may also request dental and medical records for the missing adult and even fingerprints if the missing person has had them taken for some reason (employment, security check, etc.). Finally, the police may need a personal item of the missing adult so that search dogs can use the scent to track the person.

It is also important when making a missing person report that one member of the family be designated as the contact person for the police. This will prevent family members from getting fragmented information about the case. Everyone will know who to call for information.

Also, any family members who report an adult as missing to the police should be certain to ask for a case number and also write down the name, badge number, and telephone number of the investigator who will be handling the case. This will be necessary in the event new information becomes available that needs to be passed on to the police. Also, it is crucially important to be totally honest when making the report. Many family members of missing adults know pretty well why the person left but are embarrassed to air the family's dirty laundry. However, the investigator needs the truth if he or she is going to be able to conduct a proper investigation.

Loved ones of missing adults must also be totally honest with the police about any mental problems the missing person has, including any radical changes in behavior prior to the disappearance. This could change the status of the case to endangered, and consequently warrant a much larger police response.

In addition, family members shouldn't be afraid to check in with the investigator assigned to the case from time to time or to pass along any new information that turns up, no matter how small. Family members might also want to ask the investigator what kind of help they can give. There may be things the investigator needs assistance with.

Although many missing adults are never reported, two examples can show the value of reporting missing adults to the police. In the first one, the family of twenty-nine-year-old Karla Ranee Moss-Harrigan reported her as missing from New Hanover County, North Carolina, on February 18, 2008. Her family feared for her safety because she had a medical condition that required constant medication. On March 18, 2009, however, the New Hanover County Sheriff's Department cancelled the missing person alert. Why?

The police in Arizona had stopped Karla for a traffic violation, ran her name through the NCIC computer system, and found that she had been reported as missing. According to news reports, she was in good health and "told officers she did not want to return to North Carolina."[13] While her reluctance to return home was likely known to at least some of her family and would have justified them not reporting her as missing, at least now her family members know that she is okay.

In a similar case, on the morning of March 24, 2008, Mike Mallory, the fifty-year-old owner of the Gotta Hava Java coffee shops in Glide, Oregon, left for work, but then didn't return home that evening. His wife, naturally alarmed, called the police. Officers later found Mike's pickup truck over an embankment and involved in a collision with a tree, but no sign of him in the vehicle. The police searched the area and even used a dive team to search a nearby river.

At the time of his disappearance, Mike had been in the midst of a legal fight with his parents over control of the coffee shops, which his father had founded. According to court documents, Mike's father claimed that Mike hadn't paid for the business as he'd agreed to. In

October 2008, with Mike still missing, a court gave the business back to his father.

Then, in December 2009, the U.S. Customs and Border Protection Office in San Diego notified the authorities in Oregon that they had located Mike. Because his wife had reported him as missing to the authorities, and he had appeared endangered, the police had entered his information into the FBI's NCIC computer system. The Border Patrol consequently had stopped Mike when they checked his identification through NCIC as he tried to reenter the United States from Mexico. Mike told the immigration officers that he had been living in San Diego for eight months. However, since, unlike a juvenile, there is no law against adults being missing from home, the Border Patrol had no reason to hold him.

In the two previous cases, there had been at least some evidence that these two individuals were endangered, and so the police had conducted full-blown investigations. For the majority of missing adults, though, meaning those that don't have medical or mental conditions, and who don't appear to have been the victims of foul play, there is really very little the police can or will do other than take a report and perhaps do a cursory search for the person.

"I don't think any law enforcement agency is going to dedicate those kinds of resources to track down each and every missing person without signs of a crime," said Captain Craig Rogers of the Bremerton, Washington, Police Department.[14]

But still, because of the possibility that a missing adult has actually been the victim of an accident or foul play, or the likelihood that one of these might occur after the disappearance, it is advantageous to report a missing adult to the police as soon as possible. "It's best to start looking sooner rather than later," said Richmond County, Georgia, sheriff's investigator Paul Evans.[15]

If, on the other hand, a family doesn't report a missing adult to the police, or delays for several days or weeks before doing it, and the police find a body without any identification, it can often be very difficult to identify the remains. "When a person is missing, or murdered, but no missing person's report has been filed, it is nearly impossible to identify the body," said Sergeant Paul Schiefke of the Suffolk County,

New York, police. "Who knows who they are if nobody reports them missing?"[16]

I recall a case we had when I was commander of the Indianapolis Police Department Homicide Branch. We had responded to the report of a body in the White River near the downtown area. When I arrived at the scene, the fire department was just pulling the body of a middle-aged woman out of their boat and onto the shore. The woman had been in the river, it appeared, for some time, but carried no identification. When we checked with our Missing Persons Unit they could find no reports that matched our victim. In our attempt to identify her, we put out news releases and sent information about the body everywhere we could think of. Sadly, no one ever claimed the body and we never found out who she was.

While I advise all readers who are searching for a missing adult to notify the police, there is a problem readers need to be aware of. Even if the police, after taking a report, do happen onto the missing adult, most agencies aren't allowed to tell the family where the person is, only that he or she is alive and well. For example, the website of the Mesa, Arizona, police department states, "Being a missing person is not a crime. Adults can be missing if they choose to. Because of this, law enforcement is quite limited in what they can do. Even if law enforcement does locate the person, they cannot divulge any information about that person without specific permission from that person."[17]

In a case, for example, that occurred in Seattle, an alarmed husband whose wife had suddenly disappeared reported her to the police as missing and a possible suicide threat. When Detective Christie-Lynn Bonner found the woman, however, she discovered that the missing wife had left the state and moved in with another man in southern California. "The woman was very unhappy when I found her," said Detective Bonner.[18] But because of privacy laws, all Detective Bonner could tell the husband was that his wife was alive, and nothing else.

Lieutenant Scott Buehler of the Montclair, New Jersey, police department commented on this problem with missing adults. "Once you locate someone, unless they are endangered, it's not like you can arrest and bring them somewhere against their will. There is nothing against the law [about] not wanting to be found."[19]

Still, regardless of this nondisclosure problem, it is still a good idea to report missing adults to the police in case they should turn up in an accident or as a murder victim. And, if all a person doing the searching really wants to know is that the missing adult is all right, then this nondisclosure problem is really not a problem at all.

When someone reports a missing adult to the police, there is certain information the reporting individual should have ready. As an article about finding missing persons stated, "Rule of thumb: the more information you can supply when locating missing people, the easier it becomes."[20] The reporting officer might not even ask for some of the information below, but the person making the report should give it to the officer anyway. This information includes:

1. A recent photograph and also one in profile if possible
2. Name, including nicknames, maiden names, and any aliases the person may have used
3. Date of birth
4. Sex and race
5. Height and weight
6. Eye color
7. Hair color and style when last seen
8. Any specific identifying marks, including tattoos, scars, moles, birthmarks, deformities, false teeth, cosmetic surgeries, etc.
9. Clothing the person was last seen wearing
10. Any specific identification information available, such as Social Security number, driver's license number, passport information, cell phone number, credit card information, e-mail address, etc.
11. Any serious medical conditions and any medications the missing person may be taking
12. All information possible on any vehicle the missing person may be in
13. Information on military service, in the event the missing person uses a VA hospital or applies for veteran's benefits
14. When and where the person was last seen
15. Why the person should be considered as missing

16. The missing person's physician and dentist in case verification of a body is needed
17. Any possible location the person may be heading for
18. Where the person had been employed
19. Possible reasons the person may have left
20. Any other information a loved one can think of that might assist in locating the missing person. As stated above, a loved one simply cannot supply too much information.

Readers also need to be aware that the laws in various states treat cases of adult missing persons differently. While missing children reported to the police are required by federal law to be entered into NCIC, this is not so with adults. They might be entered. They might not. Also, what happens to missing adult cases as time passes varies between states. In Oregon, for example, a law passed in 2008 requires that in cases of an adult reported missing who is not located within thirty days the investigating police agency must attempt to obtain DNA samples of the missing person (from a hairbrush, toothbrush, razor, etc.) and also collect DNA reference samples from family members. These samples are then sent to the University of North Texas Center for Human Identification, where they are analyzed and put into a national DNA database for missing persons. Following this, if the DNA sample matches that of an unidentified body already in the system, a report will be sent to the submitting police agency. If not, the sample is kept to be matched against future entries into the system. Unfortunately, not all states are as vigilant as this.

Again, as we spoke about earlier, depending on the circumstances of the disappearance, the police may or may not conduct an extensive search for a missing adult. Often, besides the conditions of the disappearance, such as indications of foul play or the missing person being in danger, the location that the adult disappears from can also make a difference in how much effort the police will put into their search for him or her. Large cities, for example, have far too many adult missing person cases every year for their police departments to assign officers to look for individuals who have left voluntarily and are not doing anything illegal by doing so.

Los Angeles, for example, with a reported 4,000 new adult missing person cases every year, has six investigators to look for them. Seattle has two detectives assigned to its missing persons unit, and handles about 500 new cases a year. In Las Vegas, a very popular place to go missing, with 12,000 new cases every year, the police department has 12 detectives assigned to its missing persons unit, which gives each investigator a whopping 1,000 new cases each year.

In smaller communities, where missing adult reports are rarer, the police may put much more effort into their search for a missing adult. Readers will recall that in the two incidents at the beginning of this chapter the police in these small communities didn't believe that foul play or imminent danger was involved, but still they mounted a considerable effort to find these people.

Usually however, the police, even if initially willing to look for a missing adult, will soon have new cases to work on and will not be able to continue the initial effort. Therefore, in most cases, the loved ones of missing adults are soon left to search on their own. So what can the loved ones of missing adults do when everyone else has stopped looking? Actually, there is a lot that can be done, and with just a little effort and perseverance the missing adults can be found.

1. The first thing that needs to be done, if not done already, is to gather as much personal information as possible about the missing adult. Along with addresses, date of birth, Social Security number, and driver's license number, searchers should also attempt to find credit card numbers, investment account numbers (the missing person will have to receive any checks from these accounts in his or her real name), and any other possible identifiers that can pinpoint someone as the missing person. Also, searchers should write down everything family members know about the missing person's lifestyle. They shouldn't discount any facts about the missing person as being inconsequential, as it could turn out to be the information that locates him or her. This information will come in handy with several of the steps I suggest below.

2. Searchers should try to honestly determine the motivation for the person disappearing. Outside love interests, for example, can often point to a location.

3. As we talked about in the chapter on finding runaway children, searchers for missing adults must also have a calm, clear mind in order to make sound, rational decisions. It is easy to become stressed and panicky when someone close suddenly and inexplicably disappears, but panic and hysteria will only interfere with the search.

4. Searchers for missing adults should keep a notebook from the start of the investigation. In this notebook loved ones should include everything done in the search, all pertinent conversations, and all contacts made. As we talked about in the chapter on runaways, this cannot only jog memories but also save considerable time in avoiding repetitions and double-backs.

5. The home of the missing adult should be searched thoroughly for any clues as to why the person left and where he or she may have gone. This includes looking for letters, e-mails, chat room discussions on a personal computer, and any instant messaging on other personal electronic devices. Searchers should also check the computer history for any map searches, and examine any photos in digital cameras. Along with what the missing person left behind, however, searchers should also try to determine what the missing person took. This may give a reason for the disappearance and/or a destination.

6. Loved ones of a missing adult should also thoroughly search the area where the missing person was last seen. As we saw in the last chapter, often adults aren't missing, but rather the victims of an accident. As a part of this, searchers should check the area for any security surveillance cameras. This is one of the first things the police do at any crime scene. These type of cameras are now installed everywhere, and may contain information about the person's disappearance.

In addition, while searchers are at the last place a missing adult was seen they should conduct a neighborhood canvass. They should knock on doors for several blocks in every direction and ask about the missing person. In every neighborhood there is almost always the neighborhood snoop who knows everything that goes on in the area. Find this person. The police, who do a canvass at most major crime scenes, often turn up very valuable clues through these individuals.

7. Another important thing to do right away with a missing adult is to have plenty of missing person posters printed, identical to the ones

we talked about in the chapter on finding runaways. In addition, the poster should be scanned into a computer for e-mailing. These will be needed because there are many places they will have to be sent. Missing adults who have left voluntarily will often change their names, but seldom their appearance. Therefore, a photograph on a missing person poster can many times jar someone's memory of a person they've seen.

8. Searchers should hang these missing person posters in high-traffic areas where people will see them, especially in transportation centers where individuals from other areas will be passing through. If possible, loved ones should also try to have them posted at interstate rest stops and at any other spot where travelers who may have seen the missing person will see the poster. The locations where these missing person fliers can be hung are limited only by the imagination of the missing person's loved ones.

In addition, searchers for missing adults should get on the Internet and send a copy of their flier to every missing-person site possible. As we have seen in this book, many missing adults have been located through information on these Internet sites. Searchers should be particularly certain to send a missing person poster and other information about the missing adult to the National Center for Missing Adults (NCMA) at www.missingadults.org or at 1-800-690-FIND, and also to the North American Missing Persons Network at www.nampn.org. These are huge sites that have many visitors every day.

9. If a missing adult has only been missing for a short time, and a personal vehicle wasn't used in the disappearance, searchers should take a copy of the missing person flier to all transportation centers in the area (airports, bus depots, train stations, etc.) to see if anyone there remembers the missing adult buying a ticket or boarding a commercial vehicle.

10. If, on the other hand, the missing adult is believed to be in a personal vehicle, searchers should be certain the police know about it. Also, the license plates will eventually have to be renewed, so it can be worthwhile to check with the Department of Motor Vehicles in any state the missing adult is suspected of being in. In addition, the dealership where the missing person purchased the car may be able to get on their computer and see if the car is being serviced somewhere.

11. Often, missing adults can disappear on a spur-of-the-moment impulse. This lack of planning can then many times lead to serious financial difficulties. Therefore, searchers should send a missing person poster to all homeless shelters in the area and, if a destination is suspected, to the shelters in that area.

12. Publicity is the best weapon available for finding missing adults. The more people that can be reached with information about missing adults the more likely it is that someone will recognize them. As I show below, and many other places in this book, many missing person cases have been solved through tips to the police from someone who saw information about missing people and then recognized them.

For example, Kristy Ormsby disappeared on June 4, 2004, leaving behind a three-year-old daughter. The day she vanished, Ormsby was supposed to have picked up her daughter and then joined her parents for dinner. However, the twenty-six-year-old didn't pick up her daughter and she didn't show up for dinner. Instead, the police believe, she left her home in Illinois with a man named James Bradstreet, who at the time was wanted for attempted murder. As can be imagined, Ormsby's family feared greatly for her safety.

A Public Service Announcement on CBS's *The Early Show* featured the Ormsby case. A viewer in North Carolina recognized her and called the authorities. The police found Ormsby living in North Carolina with James Bradstreet and a new two-month-old son.

As we discussed in the chapter on finding runaways, a spot like this on national television is worth 100,000 missing person posters. Of course, not every case can be on national television, but searchers for missing adults should try to get the information about them onto any media outlet possible. Searchers never know who will see this information.

13. A particularly effective method for locating missing adults is through the use of social networking sites, similar to what we talked about in the chapter on searching for runaways. Like teenagers, many adults are addicted to social networking, and will continue to use it even after disappearing. Therefore, searchers for missing adults should keep an eye out for activity on the social networking sites the missing adult used.

"It may be the person keeps their head down, but we can find them through their children and friends," said Mark Grover, a private detective who uses social networking to find people. "They often leave a cyber trail through their social and family connections."[21]

Also, searchers should be suspicious of any new members of these sites who sound or seem similar to the missing adult. Along with this, there are areas on most social networking sites where information on missing persons can be posted. "Never before have you been able to get information out via Facebook pages and forums and blogs and Tweets, with the capabilities of the public to get more involved in a case by being able to post their thoughts, suggestions, opinions and insights," said Corinne Geller, spokesperson for the Virginia State Police.[22]

Many families of missing persons also start their own websites. This can be very helpful because individuals regularly clicking on these sites can be updated quickly as things happen and change in the case. To be really effective though, the owners of these websites must attempt to get as many other websites as possible to link to their site.

14. Along with social networking, the loved ones of missing adults can also make use of computer search engines in their attempt to find a missing adult, particularly in finding those individuals who have been missing long enough to reestablish themselves in a new community somewhere. However, searchers must be cautious. There are a large number of these people-finder websites on the Internet that charge a fee, promise fantastic results, but deliver only meaningless data. Many of these sites are useless, if not outright scams. A lot of them will only give users a list of names similar to the one searched for, and if the missing person has a common name, then the list can be huge. Searchers must then investigate each name. But there are also some very good people-finder sites, which I will talk about below.

Before going to one of the sites I recommend below, which will charge a fee, it is probably better to first run a search for a missing adult on one of the large, free search engines, such as Google, Yahoo, or MSN. While these sites usually won't turn up a good address, they can still provide leads or point the searchers in a general direction. But the loved ones of a missing person using one of these sites must be prepared for false leads. Even unusual names can have multiple owners. Also, some information on the Internet is patently false.

If these free search engines don't provide any useable clues, then a fee-based people-finder site may turn up results. I happened onto a very effective site when I was in charge of the Homicide Branch at the Indianapolis Police Department. While in that job I found that many times individuals arrested for murder wouldn't go to trial until several years after the arrest. Unfortunately, during this time witnesses for the prosecution would often move their residence, many times without giving a forwarding address. And so, when it came time for trial, crucial witnesses would often be missing, and my detectives would have to scramble to find them, many times unsuccessfully.

One day, a man called my office at the police department and introduced himself as the representative of an Internet website called Accurint. He explained that his site accessed billions of public and private records, and could be used to locate practically anyone. To entice me, he offered a thirty-day free trial. He told me that all I needed was a name, age, and city where the person had lived. So I tried it and was astounded at how much information I could obtain with such limited input, particularly since we usually had much more personal data on the people we were trying to locate, as will the loved ones of most missing adults. A Social Security number, a date of birth, passport information, and so forth will bring even better results.

I was so impressed with the capabilities of this site that I persuaded the police department to contract with the company. Actually, the site was so effective that I found myself forced to put safeguards on its use to make sure my detectives didn't utilize it to find information on ex-spouses and lovers. Apparently, after I transferred from the Homicide Branch to the Organized Crime Branch the police department changed companies and began using a website called Locate Plus. Why I'm not sure. Readers, therefore, might find it useful to call their local police department and ask what people-finder website they use.

15. The website for the Las Vegas Metropolitan Police Department has some interesting advice for individuals searching for a missing adult: "If you have a Social Security number for the person you

are looking for, you may write a letter to the missing person, put it in an envelope with his or her name on it. Write another letter to the Social Security Administration Office explaining that you are looking for this person. Be sure to include the Social Security number of the missing person in this letter. Place both letters in an envelope to the Social Security Administration Office and ask that the enclosed letter be forwarded to the person's last known address."[23]

16. Searchers for missing adults mustn't forget to talk with extended family members, including ex-in-laws. The missing adult may have said something to them about being unhappy, about leaving, and about a possible destination because he or she didn't feel comfortable talking about it with close family members. Along with those above, searchers for a missing adult should also talk to coworkers, friends, and to everyone who knew the missing person even just a little. While these last individuals may not know anything about the missing person's whereabouts, they may know about other contacts, other people who knew the missing person that the searchers were unaware of. Often, third party contacts can provide very useful information.

An article about finding missing persons clearly states the importance of these third party contacts, "Skiptracing [locating someone who has skipped town] is done by collecting as much information as possible about a subject, which is then analyzed, reduced, and verified. Sometimes the subject's current whereabouts are in the data, but are obfuscated by the sheer amount of information and disinformation. More often, the data will be used to identify third parties that might be able to assist the process."[24]

17. If the missing person is a spouse and a Social Security number is available, a good place to look for information is credit reporting bureaus. These organizations will very possibly have a current address. Simple things such as filling out an application for a new job, turning on utilities, renting an apartment, or buying property will trigger an update to a credit report. Many private investigators try this first when looking for a missing person.

18. Voter registration databases are another good place to look for information on a missing adult. If individuals voted regularly in their

life before disappearing, they will likely continue to do so in their new life.

19. Another important database to search is the Uniform Commercial Code (UCC) filings. These are lien notices that states keep on file. They can often provide information on the location of a missing adult.

20. It can many times be helpful to look up old acquaintances of a missing adult, especially those who searchers believe haven't had contact with the missing person for some time. Occasionally, missing people will need help, but don't want to contact anyone from the life they just left, and will instead contact someone from their past.

21. As with runaways, often what adults leave behind when they disappear can tell volumes about their plans. For example, many times adults who leave without any possessions at all do so because they are not planning on needing any since they are going to end their lives. This information, of course, should be given immediately to the police.

22. Loved ones of a missing adult should contact their state missing person clearinghouse with information about the missing adult. These agencies can also provide valuable information on services available to the families of missing adults. Contact information for the various state missing person clearinghouses can be obtained from NCMA, mentioned in number 8 above.

23. Many states have websites that allow the public to search their database of prisoners in custody. Searchers should check to see if the missing adult might be in custody somewhere and, because of this, is too ashamed to contact family members. Another possible way a missing person may be incarcerated is in a mental institution, particularly if the missing person was having mental problems just before disappearing. If family members suspect this might be the case, they should send a missing person flier to as many of these institutions as they can find.

24. As we have talked about before, another possibility that must always be considered is that the missing adult may have joined some type of cult. There are thousands of cults in the United States, and

many of them do not allow their members to have contact with anyone from their previous lives. Searchers, therefore, might want to consider checking with any cult awareness groups in the area.

25. The family of a missing adult should keep a close eye on phone bills, credit and debit card statements, and ATM transactions for any use by the missing person. These transactions could point toward a destination. Also, occasionally purchases made just before the disappearance can point toward a missing person's location.

26. If a missing adult took personal electronic devices and these haven't been shut off yet, loved ones might try calling the missing person's cell phone or other electronic device periodically.

27. Searchers should keep in mind that even though missing adults may want to start a new life, they will usually base this new life on their old life. These individuals are still going to have the same likes and dislikes, they will usually still enjoy the same sports and hobbies, they will still have to take the same medicine, etc. Searchers can use this information to their advantage by contacting the various businesses and organizations that deal with these likes and dislikes.

However, searchers should keep in mind that many businesses and organizations may not want to release information about the missing person for various reasons. It could be against the law to do so. It could be against company policy. And sometimes businesses and organizations will refuse to give out the information for no particular reason at all. Searchers, therefore, may have to use a ruse to get the information, or even hire a lawyer if the information should be given out but the business or organization refuses to do so.

28. Depending on what he or she may be expecting to receive in the mail (checks, dividends, etc.), the missing adult may have put in a change of address at the post office. The missing person's stock broker and/or accountant may also have information about a new location.

29. Check the last place the missing adult worked. Is the final check being forwarded somewhere? Did he or she talk to any coworkers about disappearing or a possible destination? Also, has a new employer called to check on a reference by the missing person or has the missing person requested that a reference be sent somewhere?

30. If an adult has only been missing for a short time, a good place to search is that person's trash. Readers would be amazed at what people throw away thinking no one will see it.

31. If the missing adult was an avid reader and, as a consequence, was a subscriber to certain magazines or a member of certain book clubs, check to see if the missing person sent a change of address to them.

32. Depending on the occupation the missing adult was in, he or she may need to transfer union membership to a new location. If a license is needed to perform the missing adult's occupation, a new license or the transfer of an old one will be necessary.

33. A visit to the missing adult's doctor and dentist may prove worthwhile. Ask if a request to forward records has been made.

34. Check with the bank the missing adult used. Have accounts been closed? Have funds been transferred to another financial institution?

35. If missing adults had car loans, college loans, or other financial responsibilities that they regularly paid, they may very well continue to do so from a new location.

36. Missing adults may not have thought to take their birth certificate with them, and this is a document often needed when building a new life. Check to see if a request for a copy of the birth certificate has been made.

37. If missing adults receive any kind of federal assistance, such as VA benefits, check to see if they put in a change of address.

38. The hobbies of missing adults are unlikely to change. If individuals liked to golf, fish, hunt, or build birdhouses before they disappeared, they will likely continue to do so. Check with organizations that cater to the missing person's specific hobby. Also, check with state fish and game agencies to see if a new license has been issued.

39. The insurance company missing adults used can also be a source of information about a new location. Missing people will likely need insurance in their new location and will also likely use the same company. Also, searchers should attempt to find out where payments for previously held life or health insurance policies are now coming from.

40. If missing adults had regular prescription medicines they took, they will have to continue to do so. If these prescriptions were filled by a national chain of drugstores, check to see if the prescriptions are now being filled somewhere else.

41. Loved ones of a missing adult who are at wit's end may want to consider hiring a private investigator. This can be expensive, but as we've seen several times in this book some private investigators are extremely good at finding missing persons. Also, many private investigators have access to databases that the police and the public don't. However, before any money exchanges hands, loved ones should check out any private investigator thoroughly. Make certain he or she has experience in finding missing persons. Also, ask for references and check them out.

"The family members of a missing person will almost always receive better service from a PI than the police," private investigator Leigh Hearon told me. "The police, because of their caseloads, simply cannot give family members the personal attention that a PI can. Also, a PI isn't constrained by jurisdictional concerns and doesn't have to answer to a large bureaucracy."[25]

"I was contacted by a man who said his father had been missing for 40 years," Judd Green, a retired police officer who now works as a PI in Indianapolis, told me. He went on to tell me this story:

> He last saw his father when he was five years old and his father was backing out of the driveway and waving goodbye to him. My client said that all his life his mother had told him that his father left them and never wanted to see them again, and that's what he believed for 40 years.
>
> When my client's mother died he was going through her things and found a trunk. Inside, he discovered letters from his father as well as gifts his father had sent him over the years. After my client read the letters he realized his mother had kept the letters and gifts a secret because she was angry at his father for divorcing her. My client said he had sons now, and that he wanted me to find his father so he could try to reconnect with him, but that also he needed his father's medical history. One of my client's sons was sick and the doctor said it could be a genetic condition passed down from

grandfather to grandson, possibly skipping a generation. The doctor said he couldn't be sure of this until he reviewed the grandfather's medical history.

Obviously, the police would not be interested in this case because there was no emergency nor was there any evidence the grandfather had been the victim of a crime. He left his wife and son willingly after the divorce. Secondly, it had been so many years since the father left that the police wouldn't want to spend their limited resources finding this 'missing' man.

As far as public information sources, there are some available on the Internet, as well as records that can be searched. However, without investigative expertise and experience, it is unlikely that the untrained person will know which information is important enough to be an actual lead in locating the person being sought. I was able to locate my client's father after extensive investigative efforts. The man met personally with me later and told me what a wonderful reunion they'd had and how appreciative he was of my efforts. Obviously, this was a personally rewarding case to be involved in.[26]

While the above incident shows the value of hiring a private investigator, readers should keep in mind that if a private investigator is hired, he or she will likely want to first investigate the reasons the missing person is being searched for. Private investigators don't want to help stalkers or even murderers find their victims. A dramatic case of this occurred a number of years ago when a man named Robert John Bardo hired a private investigator to find the address of actress Rebecca Schaeffer, whom Bardo had been stalking. When the private investigator gave Bardo the address, Bardo went there and murdered Schaeffer. Private investigator Leigh Hearon told me:

A PI has to be very careful when taking a missing person case. You don't want to find out that you've helped a stalker find his or her victim. It's not the time to be shy. You must absolutely know the intent of the person or persons who want to reconnect with a family member or friend. I always apologize for seeming to be so intrusive beforehand, but I do insist on getting the full story of why someone disappeared and the reasons the client is trying to make contact now. Then I double-check as much of the story as I can.

For example, if I discover that a domestic violence protection order exists or has existed between family members, I won't touch the case. It says to me that there's a reason the missing person doesn't want to be found.[27]

42. In Indianapolis recently, the family of a missing woman named Molly Dattilo took the unusual step of suing the man they believe is responsible for her disappearance. Molly was twenty-three years old when she disappeared six years ago. The police have made no arrests in the case, and a body has never been found. Still, on November 16, 2010, a judge ordered John Shelton, who is serving time in prison on other charges, to pay the Dattilo family $3.5 million.

"It is one thing to be able to close a casket and say good bye," said Keri Dattilo, a cousin of Molly, "and it's another to never know what happened to your loved one."[28]

43. If a missing person has been gone for many years, long enough to establish a new life and new family in another community, searchers might try looking on websites such as www.ancestry.com or www.familysearch.org.

44. A possibility that unfortunately must always be considered in a missing adult case is that the person may be deceased. As we have talked about in previous chapters, as of November 2009, over 40,000 sets of unidentified human remains sat in medical examiner and coroner's offices across the United States. In the past, families were forced to call every coroner's office and every medical examiner's office individually to see if a body there matched their missing loved one. Fortunately, that is no longer the case. There is now one Internet site that brings all of these offices together.

Loved ones of missing adults should contact the National Missing and Unidentified Persons System (NamUs) at www.namus.gov. This website contains two large sets of data. One set gives the details of various missing person cases in the United States. The other gives information about unidentified human remains sitting in morgues across the country. Law enforcement and other governmental agencies can add data about a missing person case and can also search for potential matches. But more important to readers, this site, which came online in

2009, is also open to the public. Family members and others can enter as much information as they have on a missing person and then see if a possible match comes up.

"The concept of NamUs and the ability to bring the different disciplines together to share information is extremely important," said P. Michael Murphy, coroner for Clark County, Nevada. "The real component that makes it so successful, in my opinion, is the ability to give families search capability."[29] This search capability can empower the families of missing persons to become part of the solution.

Alice Beverly did just that with information she had about her sister Paula Beverly Davis, who disappeared in 1987. She logged onto NamUs and found that Paula's body had turned up in another state only days after she had disappeared, but no one then knew who she was. Alice recognized Paula through several tattoos the body had. "I just broke down crying instantly," said Alice. "It was like, 'We found her!'"[30]

The idea for this database came from the 9/11 tragedy, when the many problems of identifying human remains became very apparent. Authorities realized that a centralized system was needed. "Instead of having this fragmented system where people go to coroners, to medical examiners, to law enforcement, we have everything in a central depository," said Katrina Rose of the National Institute of Justice.[31]

45. There are many support groups available for the loved ones of missing persons. If searchers feel the need for this support, the names of these organizations can usually be obtained through local social service agencies.

46. Finally, family members and friends of missing adults should never, never give up hope. As we have already seen and as the following anecdotes show, missing people can be located years and even decades after disappearing.

Erick Wales, twenty-four-years-old, worked as an information technology specialist at a San Diego television station. On April 19, 2010, he disappeared, much to the surprise and anguish of his family. The police later found his black Saturn Ion abandoned under an Interstate in Barrio Logan, a neighborhood on the south side of San Diego.

This, of course, worried his family even more. Had he been kidnapped? Was he still alive?

Once the police had located Erick's car, a website started by his family contained the following statement: "Unanswered questions still exist, but to be clear—we have NOT found Erick Wales. Erick needs our help to return home safely to his family and friends that love and care for him. We ask that you keep posting flyers."[32]

In November 2010, a tip to the police allowed them to finally locate Erick. Apparently, he had decided he wanted to move to a new community and start a new life, but hadn't told anyone about it.

Upon the discovery of his new location by the police, Erick's family posted the following message on their website: "He has established himself in another community and has chosen to pursue the course that he is on and his new direction."[33]

Nicholas Francisco, a twenty-eight-year-old ad executive who lived in the Seattle/Tacoma area, told his coworkers on February 13, 2008, that he was headed for the local Safeway supermarket and then home to bake Valentine cookies with his pregnant wife and two children. Following this, he disappeared. Several days later, the police discovered his red 1992 Toyota Paseo abandoned in Federal Way, a suburb of Tacoma. Fearing foul play, the authorities launched an investigation and search. They even brought in tracking dogs to look for a scent in case Nicholas had been taken by force from his car.

Nicholas's mother, Rosann Francisco, came to the scene where the police had found Nicholas's car. "I've only been praying that if someone is persecuting my son, I pray for their heart to be softened so that my son can be brought back to us safely," she said.[34]

Hundreds of people joined in the effort to find Nicholas. They took part in search parties and also helped post missing person fliers. But no sign of Nicholas turned up.

Afterward, even though the police reported several possible sightings of Nicholas, they couldn't confirm them. At first at least, Nicholas's wife, Christine, believed that her husband must be in some kind of trouble because she felt certain he would never abandon his family.

"My husband would fight so hard to come home to us, and I will do the same for him," said Christine.[35]

Eventually, though, Christine began to think differently and finally filed for divorce from Nicholas, citing willful abandonment and domestic violence as her grounds. Part of the reason Christine changed her mind and filed for divorce was that the police investigation into Nicholas's disappearance turned up evidence that he had been leading a secret life while married to Christine, including having several hidden bank accounts.

"He had been leading a horrific double life since before we were married, and I never knew of it," said Christine.[36]

Finally, almost two years after Nicholas's disappearance, a reporter for a local television station finally found him. Nicholas had been living in Los Angeles and going by the name Alex Martin. The reporter asked Nicholas about abandoning his wife and now three children. "You know, it's sad that I can't be a part of that," Nicholas told the reporter, "but I don't want to be around for the rest of that. There's a whole (expletive) ecosystem around that I don't even care for."[37]

At the divorce hearing, a court had ordered Nicholas to pay $906 a month in child support. At the time of his discovery, he was $16,321 in arrears.

In 1986, twenty-seven-year-old Keri Bray, a mentally disabled man who lived at the Lake Crest Development Center in Orem, Utah, told the workers there that he wanted to go to Texas and become a cowboy. Soon afterward, Keri walked out of the center with only the clothing he had on and then vanished. The center reported his disappearance to the police. Because of Keri's mental condition, the police feared that he wouldn't be able to look after himself, so they conducted a full-scale search. But they found no trace of him and eventually suspected that he may have died.

The missing person case fell to Lieutenant Denton Johnston of the Orem Police Department. Because of Keri's disability, Lieutenant Johnston took the case personally and kept investigating it for years.

"In a missing person case, you can't just close it, because there's a human being missing," Lieutenant Johnston said. "It's kind of like a homicide investigation, you leave it open forever if necessary."[38]

Twenty-one years after Keri's disappearance, a cowboy crashed a tractor on a ranch in Texas. The cowboy had worked at the ranch for twenty-one years. The insurance adjuster wanted to find out more about the cowboy and did a Google search on his name. He was directed to the Doe Network, a website for long-term missing people. On the website, the insurance adjuster found the picture of a man who had disappeared from Orem, Utah, twenty-one years before. He was certain it was the cowboy. After finding that the cowboy's name and date of birth were the same as those of the man listed on the Doe Network, the insurance adjuster notified the Orem Police Department.

"It's kind of a fun story," Lieutenant Johnston, now retired, said. "It made me feel good today. That's a long time that he's been gone."[39]

This incident shows that missing adults can often be found long after they disappear. Consequently, searchers should never get so discouraged that they believe these individuals will never be found.

As readers who keep up on current events know, the newspapers in early 2011 were filled with stories about how the first Baby Boomers were turning 65. The stories told about how census figures showed that America is becoming grayer and grayer as medical advances help people live longer lives. However, as we will see in the next chapter, along with this aging of America comes the problem of a loss of mental acuity for many of its elderly citizens, which can cause these individuals to suddenly become the missing elderly.

· 9 ·

The Problem of the Missing Elderly

"*O*ld people with dementia have a duty to die and should be pushed towards death."

The above is the headline for the September 20, 2008, issue of *Mail Online*, a British publication. The story concerns an interview that Baroness Mary Warnock, a leading expert on medical ethics, gave to the Church of Scotland's magazine *Life and Work*.[1] In a similar article published in the September 18, 2008, issue of the British newspaper the *Telegraph*, she is also quoted as saying, "If you're demented, you're wasting people's lives—your family's lives—and you're wasting the resources of the National Health Service."[2]

Fortunately, Baroness Warnock's stance appears to be in the minority. Phyllis Bowman, executive director of the group Right to Life, appalled by Baroness Warnock's statements, responded, "It sends a message to dementia sufferers that certain people think they don't count, and that they are a burden on their families. It's a pretty uncivilized society where that is the primary consideration."[3]

In a further rebuttal of Baroness Warnock's stance, and as the following anecdotes show, most elderly people, many of them with dementia, are treasured by their loved ones and by the public at large. This is shown by the loved one's concern when these individuals become lost, and by the community's commitment to finding them through the extremely manpower-intensive searches put together by law enforcement and citizen volunteers.

Denzle Stanley, an eighty-four-year-old man, reportedly suffered from Alzheimer's disease, a type of dementia. On January 5, 2011, he left his home in Albany, Ohio, to walk his dog. The dog returned home, but without Denzle. Because of Denzle's disability, and the fact that he apparently hadn't been dressed for January weather in Ohio, a number of local public safety agencies, a nonprofit search team from Columbus, Ohio, called Rapid Assistance to Community Emergencies, and dozens of volunteers from Denzle's neighborhood began an extensive search for him. In just three days, the search had put in 2,616 man hours, and wasn't ready to quit.

Along with volunteers and police officers on foot searching through woods and brush, the effort to find Denzle also included aircraft with thermal-imaging equipment, four-wheel off-road vehicles, officers on horseback, and even scent-tracking dogs. These dogs picked up Denzle's scent and followed it into the city of Athens, Ohio, a little over ten miles to the northeast. Then it disappeared.

"I haven't slept, haven't eaten," said Stephanie Hager, Denzle's granddaughter. "I've just been crying the whole time, hoping, hoping he would walk through the door one night."[4]

But while the large-scale search with civilian volunteers finally ended, the police still haven't given up their search for Denzle. "This case will never be closed until we get a recovery," promised Athens County sheriff's lieutenant Bryan Cooper.[5]

Dot Omelite became frantic when her eighty-eight-year-old aunt, Anna Mary Pandolph of Irwin, Pennsylvania, a suburb of Pittsburgh, suddenly turned up missing in November of 2009. Because of Anna's age and the inclement weather in Pennsylvania in November, the police immediately launched an intensive search for her. Search and rescue teams scoured the neighborhood for hours looking for the elderly woman, using police officers, volunteers from the community, and search dogs. Finally, a neighbor walking his dog stopped to see what all of the commotion was about and learned of the disappearance. He immediately recalled seeing an elderly woman sitting in a car in a driveway several doors down from Anna's home. It turned out to be Anna, who reportedly thought she was in her daughter's car and was waiting to go somewhere. Naturally, her family was elated at her safe return.

"I thank God. I thank Jesus. And I thank St. Anthony," said Dot. "I prayed the whole way here from Greensburg."[6]

As anyone who keeps up with the results of our country's censuses knows, America's population is definitely getting older and grayer. During the twentieth century, for example, the number of Americans sixty-five and older increased elevenfold, while the number of those under sixty-five only tripled.[7] According to the 2010 census, one out of every eight Americans, or over 40 million people, is age sixty-five or older. By 2030, census officials believe, one in every five Americans will be a senior citizen. The Census Bureau also projects that by 2050 the number of Americans sixty-five and older will have reached more than 88 million.[8]

While, of course, Americans have the many advances in science and medicine to thank for this increase in our country's elderly population, this extra longevity can come with a cost. With advancing age also comes the possibility of dementia.

According to national statistics, dementia is present in about 1 percent of individuals age sixty to sixty-four, yet affects as many as 30 to 50 percent of those over eighty-five.[9] The U.S. Congress Office of Technology Assessment estimates that as many as 6.8 million Americans suffer from dementia.[10]

Doctors once called dementia senility and considered it just a natural part of aging, but researchers now know that it is not, but rather that dementia is a condition that can sometimes be reversed. Dementia is not a disease in itself, and doesn't have a single cause. Dementia instead is a term that describes a variety of symptoms that can be caused by a number of things. According to the Cleveland Clinic, a major medical treatment and research center, dementia has over fifty different causes. Dementia can be caused, for example, by several diseases, by certain drugs, by head trauma, by strokes, and even by nutritional deficiencies.[11]

But of course, the most well-known cause of dementia is Alzheimer's disease, a malady named after Dr. Alois Alzheimer, a German physician who first described the disease in 1906. Doctors used to believe that the dementia that accompanies Alzheimer's was caused by a buildup of plaque in the brain, but recent research has called that into question. Regardless, though, of the cause of the dementia, Alzheimer's disease, according to the Cleveland Clinic, accounts for 50 to 70 percent of all dementia cases.[12] And, just as disturbing, statistics show that 60 percent of those with Alzheimer's disease will eventually wander away from home or some other location and become lost.[13] Unfortunately, the probability of wandering for those with other types of dementia is also dismal.

Some of the symptoms of dementia include forgetfulness (including a loss of both short- and long-term memory), difficulty performing familiar daily tasks, changes in behavior and personality, and confusion and disorientation. This confusion and disorientation can often cause those suffering from dementia to become lost, even in familiar territory, because landmarks suddenly no longer look familiar to them. Consequently, this can cause the elderly with dementia to wander away from home and become lost. And with their decreased reasoning ability and the natural frailty that comes with advancing age, their chances of coming to harm increase greatly.

Naturally, a person doesn't have to have dementia to become lost. It can happen to anyone. Individuals without dementia, and of any age, can become confused and not know where they are or how to get to some place. It's happened to me and to probably every reader at some time. However, as the following anecdotes demonstrate, for the elderly, because of their natural frailty due to aging, getting lost, particularly somewhere remote where they must walk long distances or be out in frigid weather, can often have fatal consequences.

A neighbor reported eighty-three-year-old Ann Marie Vlahovich missing on February 2, 2010. All the police knew was that she had last been seen on January 20 driving away from her San Jose, California, home in a 2001 Cadillac STS. Although the authorities conducted an extensive search for her, they didn't find any trace of Ann Marie or her vehicle. Then in April 2010, a highway work crew found Ann Marie's car off the road in the Santa Cruz Mountains about twenty-five miles from her home. The police discovered human remains near the vehicle that turned out to be those of Ann Marie. No one is sure what she was doing in the area, but she may have been lost. The authorities theorize that, after leaving the road, Ann Marie got out of her vehicle and began walking, but succumbed to her injuries and the January weather.

Witnesses last saw eighty-seven-year-old Dora Edmonson on January 8, 2011, at the Chase Bank in Lyons, Texas, a suburb of Houston. She had been seen there driving a green 1997 Ford Escort. No one saw her after that, and her family reported her as missing to the police.

"You think about foul play, but you just hope that's not the case," said Dora's granddaughter Dynise Jones. "It was cold and wet and I was just hoping that she was safe and somewhere dry, even if she is in her car pulled over somewhere, just not out in the elements like that."[14]

However, Dynise's worst fears came true. Apparently, Dora's car ran off the road and into a drainage ditch about sixteen miles from where she had last been seen. No one knows why she was there. After running off the road, and apparently unable to free her car, Dora got out and started walking, but soon fell victim to the elements and died. The police found her car and her body two days after her family had reported her as missing.

Lelia Carper, a ninety-five-year-old woman who lived in Knoxville, Tennessee, loved cats and had several of them. Because of this, she was known affectionately in her neighborhood as "The Cat Lady." On December 4, 2010, one of her cats got out of the house and she went looking for it. She didn't return.

The police and Lelia's neighbors conducted an extensive neighborhood search for her, and also passed out dozens of fliers with her picture on them. However, it wasn't until two days later that they found Lelia's body in the yard next door to her house. The police believe that she had likely become disoriented and couldn't find her way back home. The weather the night Lelia disappeared had dropped into the 20s. Naturally, all those involved in the search were disappointed.

"I thought we'd find her alive," said a neighbor who had helped in the search. "We went all the way down to First Creek, all the way to Cherry Street, driving with flashlights."[15]

As the incidents in this chapter illustrate, elderly people present a crucially time-sensitive problem when they become missing persons. Because of their frailty, they can quickly fall victim to the elements if they become lost in harsh weather or in remote locations. Consequently, beginning an immediate and thorough search for the missing elderly is imperative if there is to be any chance of finding them alive. In the next chapter, we will discuss just how to conduct such a search.

Finding the Missing Elderly

$\mathcal{N}$inety-one-year-old Mary Schulz lived at the Brentwood Assisted Living Facility in Niles, Michigan. Workers at the home knew that she didn't suffer from dementia or have a history of wandering off. Consequently, they had no concerns when she signed herself out of the facility on July 8, 2010. However, when she didn't return that night or contact her family about where she would be, they called the police and reported her as missing. The healthcare workers were especially concerned due to the fact that Mary was on daily medication that she had left in her room at the facility.

Because of Mary's age, medicine needs, and the fact that she had to use a walker to get around, the authorities mounted an immediate search. The search party was made up of the Niles Police Department, including its reserve officers and K-9 unit, the Niles Fire Department, a search-and-rescue organization called the Mutual Aid Box Alarm System/Tactical Search and Rescue Team, a number of civilian volunteers, and even the fire department from St. Joseph County across the border in Indiana.[1]

Sixty-five hours later, the authorities recovered Mary alive but injured in a densely wooded area of Niles. A man had spotted Mary's walker out behind an apartment building.

"I thought it was a bicycle at first," said Steve Alexander, talking about seeing Mary's walker, "but then I saw a purse and I knew something wasn't right."[2]

Mary had apparently fallen down a steep embankment, but had survived. How or why she was there the police didn't know. When they found her she could only tell them her name and no more. Fortunately, this event occurred during warm weather or it likely would have had a tragic ending.

Florence L. Leatherman, an eighty-four-year-old woman with dementia, lived with her son in Maryland. On December 15, 2009, her son returned home to find his mother missing. After Florence's family had searched the home and surrounding area, Florence's son reported her as missing to the police. Because of the weather and Florence's mental and physical condition, the police immediately launched a large-scale search for her. The search party included members of the Maryland State Police, the State Police Aviation Command, the Frederick County Sheriff's Department, the Maryland Natural Resources Police, the Frederick City Police, the Frederick County Fire Department, Mid-Atlantic Search Dogs, Chesapeake Search Dogs, Susquehanna Search and Rescue, and the Thurmont K-9 Search and Rescue Unit.[3]

Fortunately, several members of the Maryland State Police had been trained in tracking and they noticed some missing patches of dew on the ground. They followed these to some property about a quarter of a mile from Florence's home. There they found Florence lying on the ground, huddled against some scrap plywood. The temperature that night had dropped to thirty degrees.

"It's a pretty amazing story," Lieutenant Michael Brady of the Maryland State Police said of Florence's rescue.[4]

The searchers bundled Florence in some blankets and had her checked out by an Emergency Medical Technician. They then sent her to a local hospital as a precaution.

"It was a total team effort," said Lieutenant Brady. "The search went exceptionally well. Everyone worked together well."[5]

What these two anecdotes have in common, besides successful outcomes, is that they were large-scale, coordinated efforts that began immediately. The missing elderly, because of their physical and often mental frailty, can many times be in grave danger when they are lost and wandering on their own. This danger, of course, is greatly multiplied whenever the elderly become lost in inclement weather. While we have talked in earlier chapters about searches for runaways and missing adults that were successfully concluded months or even years after the person disappeared, this very likely won't happen with a missing elderly person. Of all the missing people we have talked about so far in this book, the missing elderly are the most vulnerable, and the search for them must be immediate and intense if the outcome is going to be a happy one. Statistics have shown that if the missing elderly are not found within twenty-four hours, the odds of finding them alive drop to less than half. If the missing elderly are not found within seventy-two hours, they have only a one-in-five chance of being found alive.[6]

While the searches above were conducted by police and fire departments, often with the assistance of professional search-and-rescue teams, this doesn't mean that the family members of the missing elderly don't have a part in any search and rescue effort. Actually, there is much that the family can do.

The first thing that the family should do as soon as they discover an elderly person is missing is to conduct an immediate search of the home and nearby property to be certain the elderly person really is missing and not just someplace that the family didn't think to look. Locations that aren't used much, such as laundry rooms and storage areas in apartment buildings, should be checked. On private property, areas such as storage sheds, basements, and any closed-off rooms need to be searched. Naturally, if the person has wandered away before, the location he or she went to should be checked. Also, property close to the elderly person's home should be searched. According to the Alzheimer's Association, and as the following anecdote shows, 95 percent of individuals with Alzheimer's who wander away are found within a quarter-mile of their place of residence or the last place they were seen.[7]

Violet Reinsager, a ninety-four-year-old woman, lived in Muscatine, Iowa. At around 8:00 AM on January 14, 2010, she wandered away from her home, and her family reported her as missing. Because of the inclement weather in Iowa during January, the authorities feared that she could succumb to the elements. Consequently, the Iowa State Patrol, the Muscatine City Police, the Muscatine County Sheriff's Department, and the Muscatine Fire Department mounted an immediate search for her. But also joining in the effort were a number of civilian volunteers.

"I received an automated phone call from the police, asking to check the surrounding of my house and out building," said neighbor Jan Pohl, explaining how she joined the search team.[8]

At around 2:00 PM a sigh of relief could be heard in the neighborhood when the police announced that they had found Violet. She had been sitting inside a neighbor's heated porch just a few doors down from her home. Searchers said that she couldn't be seen until she stood up. Medics on the scene examined her and found her to be in good health.

The search by family members of the home and adjoining property, as advised above, shouldn't take more than fifteen or twenty minutes and could save everyone a lot of time and effort. However, once family members are certain that an elderly person actually is missing they should contact the police. During the call family members should be sure to advise the police dispatcher of any physical and/or mental problems the elderly person may have. In addition, they should be certain that the officers who respond to the call also understand the gravity of the search. If the elderly person has a serious medical or mental condition, or is especially frail, family members must tell the responding officers about this. Police officers have a great deal of resources available, and family members want to be certain that the police use all of these.

Family members will also be required to provide the police dispatcher and responding officers with an accurate description of the missing person, similar to the information talked about for missing adults in chapter 8, including what the missing elderly person was wearing when last seen. In addition, a good quality photograph or set of photographs should be available for the first responding officers, along with a list of former addresses, places of employment, and the addresses of relatives' and friends' homes. These are all places, experience has shown, where a wandering elderly person with dementia could be headed. Also, any special or secret places that the person may have liked to go to in the past should be included on the list.

Naturally, all of this will be much easier and less stressful if the family of a missing elderly person already has all of the information they will need written down somewhere and readily accessible. To facilitate this, a copy of an Adult-at-Risk Identification Card, which contains all of the information the police will need, can be downloaded from www.miami-police.org/docs/Imminent_Rescue_Adult_Brochure.pdf. Filling this card out ahead of time and then keeping it somewhere easily accessible could save precious minutes that the authorities could use for searching.

"I have been on many calls when a senior or individual with a cognitive disorder wandered," said retired Clearwater, Florida, police officer Neil Arfmann. "Time is of the essence when attempting to locate and recover these individuals. I would get frustrated when precious moments were wasted while a caregiver went looking for a current photo and vital information, when I could have been out looking for them."[9]

Officer Arfmann's frustration eventually convinced him to start a program through which vital personal information about an elderly person can be stored free of charge on a secure, encrypted website, making it readily available when emergency personnel need it. The site he developed is able to store photographs and also information about an elderly person's health, medicine needs, vehicles, and other data that could help emergency responders find the person if he or she becomes missing. The site can be accessed at www.nationalsilveralert.org or at 1-866-840-3639.

Along with having vital information readily available, it is also a good idea for caretakers to put names, addresses, and telephone numbers in the clothing of elderly people with dementia. This way if these individuals are found wandering somewhere, they can be identified and their family notified.

Once all of the relevant information about the missing elderly has been given to the police, a very important step that should be taken right away is to have one person designated by the family as the contact person for the search effort. All information should flow through this person. In this way, new leads can be passed on quickly, and the information coming into the family won't be fragmented by coming through multiple sources.

An important point to consider in any search for the elderly is how long they have been missing and their likely mode of travel. Naturally, if an elderly person has been missing for less than an hour and is on foot, the search area is much smaller than it would be if he or she is in a vehicle or has been gone much longer. Therefore, the search for a missing elderly person on foot who has been gone for less than an hour should start and then spread out from the immediate neighborhood. An important point to remember is that individuals with dementia don't always follow paved roadways or sidewalks, but will often cross them and proceed instead through bushes and thickets.

Family members of the missing elderly need to put together a missing person poster as quickly as possible. These fliers, similar to the ones talked about in earlier chapters, should include several photographs, along with a detailed list of physical identifiers, including the clothing the elderly person was last seen wearing. Also, family members should be certain to include information about any medical conditions the person may have and the missing person's state of mind (easily confused, dementia, etc.). In the event the search for the missing elderly person becomes a large-scale incident involving multiple agencies and civilian volunteers, each person will need one of these fliers.

But not everyone in the search party should be out looking for the missing elderly person. A part of the search party should begin knocking on every door within two blocks surrounding the last place the elderly person was seen. These canvassers should give the individuals they speak with one of the missing person posters and ask if they have seen the person. Quite often, people will have seen an elderly person walking by their house and not think much about it. If searchers get no information within this two-block radius, they should then expand their canvass out a block. This is an extremely important part of any search because if someone has seen the missing elderly person, then the searchers will be able to determine a direction of travel and move the search effort in that heading. Once a direction of travel has been determined, some of the searchers should spread out and look for the person in this new heading, while others should canvass along the direction of travel, looking for more information.

It is important that some of the searchers be on foot so that they can check hidden areas, but other searchers should be in vehicles cruising the surrounding streets. In addition, if the missing elderly person can still function socially, even on a decreased level, someone should check the bus and train depots, and also notify local taxi cab companies. Often, elderly people, particularly those suffering from dementia, are trying to get to somewhere from their past, and they may have used a bus, train, or taxi to do so in the past. A missing person poster should be given to these companies so that their employees can be on the lookout for the missing elderly person. Along with transportation centers, local hospitals should also be notified in case the missing person has been brought there.

A point family members of a missing elderly person should keep in mind is that the news media can be of tremendous help in finding a missing person. Therefore, family members should be certain to send a missing person flier to all news media outlets right away. Involving the news media can add thousands of eyes to the search effort.

Another possible resource for families to consider is the use of a professional, nonprofit search-and-rescue team such as Texas Equu-Search, an organization that has been involved in over 300 successful search and rescue operations. As we have seen in the incidents above, searches for the missing elderly often involve these types of organizations.

A crucial point to consider in any search for the missing elderly, however, is that if in the area the person could have wandered into there are any significant hazards, such as retention ponds or dense woods, these areas need be checked right away. Searchers should look for any clues that the missing person may have traveled this way. Family members should also discuss with the police, if the idea hasn't already been brought up, about using tracking dogs to find the missing person.

Family members and searchers should keep in mind that in good weather the missing elderly will likely continue traveling to wherever they believe is their destination. In bad weather, though, these individuals may instead find someplace to huddle in order to stay warm, which will make them harder to find, as these locations may be in dense brush or in some type of unused building.

So far in this chapter we have been talking about finding missing elderly people who are on foot. If, on the other hand, the missing elderly are driving a vehicle, then finding them can be much more difficult because, as the following anecdotes show, they can travel long distances in a short time.

Ninety-two-year-old Arturo Morales of Cameron County, Texas, had a doctor's appointment on January 18, 2011. Even at his advanced age, he liked to show his independence, and so he jumped into his 1993 Oldsmobile and took off without waiting for his daughter, who was supposed to go to the doctor with him. Unfortunately, he soon became lost.

"I couldn't find the doctor," Arturo later said. "I couldn't find the street so I just got on the highway looking to the sides to see if I could see the street. All of a sudden, I was in Brownsville [Texas]."[10]

Eventually, Arturo got onto the Pharr Bridge and crossed into Mexico. Fortunately, when he tried to come back into the United States, a Customs agent checked and found that there had been a Silver Alert (which we will talk about below) put out for him. The Customs agent notified the authorities where Arturo lived, and his family came and picked him up, ending a 500-mile journey.

In a very similar story, on November 12, 2010, an eighty-six-year-old man from Glen Rock, New Jersey, left a relative's house in his 1991 Honda Accord. As he headed for his home he became lost. When he didn't arrive home as he should have, his wife notified the police. The Connecticut State Police located him thirty hours later almost 150 miles from his home. They found him sitting in his car along the side of the road, out of gas.

As I mentioned in the incident involving Arturo Morales, a Silver Alert can be issued for a missing elderly person. This program, which is modeled after the very successful Amber Alert program for abducted children, also uses the news media, telephone alerts, and electronic highway signs to notify citizens of the missing elderly. These electronic highway signs can be particularly helpful when the elderly person is driving a car because they can alert thousands of other drivers to be on the lookout for the missing person's vehicle.

So far, as of December 2010, twenty-eight states have adopted the Silver Alert program. Each state has a slightly different protocol for activating a Silver Alert, but in most states a missing elderly person must be in danger and have some sort of mental disability. Some states, though, have resisted embracing Silver Alerts out of fear that too many alerts will dilute the effectiveness of Amber Alerts. These states fear that too many alerts will make the public apathetic about them. However, in an early study of the effectiveness of Silver Alerts, the state of North Carolina issued 151 alerts in two years, and in all but six of these cases the authorities located the missing elderly person alive.[11]

"You can put hundreds of cops on the road searching for them, and it does only so much good," said Trumbull, Connecticut Police Chief Thomas H. Kiely about Silver Alerts. "But the second you broadcast this alert on TV, radio, the electronic highway signs, and even the Internet, on a newspaper's Web site, you exponentially increase the number of people looking out for this person—and increase the odds of finding him."[12]

As the following anecdotes show, the Silver Alert program can often be very helpful in finding the missing elderly.

In Gainesville, Florida, seventy-two-year-old Betty Tomci, a dementia sufferer, who was believed to be in her car, suddenly disappeared, and as a result the police instituted a Silver Alert for her. Hours later, a clerk at a BP filling station saw her in the parking lot outside, appearing confused and disoriented. The clerk kept her there and called the police, who, because of the Silver Alert, knew who she was. She told responding police officers that she didn't know where she was, but that she was headed for Pennsylvania.

"He did exactly what he should have done—seeing a problem and calling for help," said Gainesville Police Department spokesperson Tscharna Senn, talking about the clerk's actions. "I shudder to think what could have happened if she had gotten back into her car."[13]

In another incident, this one also in Florida (the state with the highest percentage of elderly citizens), Susan M. Petras, a woman suffering from dementia, drove away from her home in Boca Raton and disappeared. The police issued a Silver Alert for her, and two days later a police officer in Key West, Florida, checked on a license plate and found that a Silver Alert had been issued for it. He stopped the car and Susan told the officer that she "went for a drive and ended up in Key West."[14] This was a 200 mile drive.

Similar to the Silver Alert program, a number of localities are now also using the A Child Is Missing program to help find the missing elderly. This program, based in Fort Lauderdale, Florida, has been very successful in finding young children who have become lost, and has now been expanded to include the missing elderly. When activated, the program calls hundreds of homes and businesses surrounding the last place the missing elderly person was seen and gives a description of the person. The program has the capability of placing up to 1,000 telephone calls a minute.

An interesting example of this program working successfully occurred in Maryland in October of 2010. A sixty-year-old woman suffering from dementia went missing. The A Child Is Missing program placed over 1,100 telephone calls in the area around the woman's home. One of the people receiving this call notified the police that she had seen the missing woman, and advised them that the woman was in jail in an adjoining jurisdiction. Apparently, the missing woman had wandered into a store and then refused to leave. The store manager called the police.

Some cities in the states that have rejected the idea of Silver Alerts have instituted their own programs to help find the missing elderly. In New York City, for example, when an elderly person is missing the authorities send out a notice to all subscribers of their "Notify NYC Alert System." This is an alert system that advises subscribers of road hazards, school closings, and other matters of public interest. But in addition to putting out this alert, when an elderly person is missing in New York City the authorities also notify all taxi cab drivers so that they can be on the lookout for the person.

The city of Amarillo, Texas, uses another very effective system for alerting the public about a missing elderly person. They use the "E-Mail Alert System," a program that regularly delivers police-related information, such as crime alerts, crime prevention tips, and requests for help in finding missing children and elderly adults, to its e-mail subscribers. Other cities use their extensive video monitoring systems to look for the missing elderly. For example, an effort was underway recently in Hawaii to use facial recognition technology (a computer system that digitizes faces seen on video and then compares them with digitized faces stored in its memory) to help in the search for the missing elderly.

Also, as we discussed in the chapter on finding runaways, family members can purchase clothing, jewelry, and other items for the elderly that contain GPS tracking devices. Using these, if an elderly person suddenly becomes missing, he or she can be located within seconds. A few of the companies that manufacture these items are EmFinders, Aetrex Company, and Project Lifesaver. There is usually a monitoring fee connected with these items, but many communities have financial help for those in need.

"We will not turn anyone away for lack of finances," said Martha LaForest, coordinator for the Project Lifesaver Program at the Cape Coral, Florida Police Department.[15]

Occasionally, as we talked about in the chapter on finding missing adults, the missing elderly may leave a credit card trail. For example, in Auburn, Maine, in September 2010, an eighty-three-year-old man became confused while driving his car and got lost. His wife reported his disappearance to the police, who found the missing man through his use of a credit card at a gas station.

Along with everything we've talked about so far, a very important point that must be considered with any missing elderly person is that the person may not be missing at all. As the following incidents demonstrate, he or she may instead have been the victim of a crime.

Family members reported eighty-one-year-old Ethel Simpson as missing in September 2010. Just before she went missing, friends had seen her driving around with thirty-nine-year-old James Cobb Hutto, a man the police were looking for on a charge of failure to register as a sex offender. Ethel had reportedly met James at the Baptist Healthflex, a recreational facility in Clinton, Mississippi. He allegedly told her that he had cancer and no family, and so she befriended him.

On September 13, 2010, witnesses saw Ethel and James together at a Vicksburg, Mississippi, casino. After that, Ethel disappeared. On September 17, 2010, the police found a body in Edwards, Mississippi, which turned out to be Ethel. She had died from a severe beating to her head and neck. The police arrested James the same day they discovered the body, stopping him as he drove Ethel's 2002 Mercedes. They charged him with Capital Murder.

"This individual is obviously suspected of some extremely serious crimes, so it's good that he's not out on the street victimizing anyone else," said Lee County Sheriff Jay Jones, whose department arrested Hutto.[16]

In a similar incident, this one in Leesburg, Florida, eighty-one-year-old Janet Patrick left her home in Leesburg to shop for groceries at the local Publix supermarket. On surveillance video she can be seen talking with fifty-year-old Donald Williams, a convicted sex offender. On the tape it appears that he helps her with her groceries and then walks out of the store with her. After that, Janet disappeared. This was on October 18, 2010.

The police discovered a body several days later in Polk County, Florida. An autopsy showed it to be that of Janet Patrick, who had also been beaten to death. The police had earlier stopped Donald as he was driving Janet's car. They found several of her credit cards in his wallet. Donald told the police that Janet had given him a ride home and that during the ride a man carjacked them and beat Janet to death. The police, however, didn't buy into this story.

"We don't believe there is an unknown suspect who carjacked them," said Lieutenant John Herrell of the Lake County Sheriff's Department.[17]

The two incidents above aside, the point of this chapter is that in dealing with the missing elderly finding them quickly is essential to finding them alive. This is particularly true for those with mental disabilities and those out in inclement weather.

If, however, a missing elderly person isn't found within a week, family members must give serious consideration to the idea that he or she may be deceased. In this event, the family should follow the advice given in chapter 8 about dealing with the possibility of a deceased missing person.

Finally, while searching for a runaway child or a missing adult can be extremely stressful, hunting for a missing elderly person can be even worse. Unlike runaways and missing adults, who often have a plan of where to go, the missing elderly many times wander off with a belief they are heading for an old location, but instead will become disoriented and lost. Because of their age and frailty, they must be found quickly if the outcome is to be happy.

A Final Thought

$\mathcal{A}$s we have seen through the many success stories reported in this book, missing people can be found. Family members and loved ones of the missing are not powerless, but instead have many tools and resources with which to find these individuals. Searchers, to be successful, simply must never give up hope and must continue the activities that are most likely to bring their loved one home. Anyone who uses the information in this book and refuses to give up trying will likely be successful in locating a missing loved one.

Notes

CHAPTER 1

1. Edgar Sandoval and Corky Siemaszko, "Missing Boy Francisco Hernandez Jr., 13, Lives in Subway System for 11 Days," *NYDailyNews.com*, 24 November 2009, www.nydailynews.com/ny_local/2009/11/24/2009-11-24_missing_boy_ francisco_hernandez_jr_13_lives_in_subway_system_for_11_days.html (accessed 6 January 2010).

2. Sandoval and Siemaszko, "Missing Boy."

3. Kirk Semple, "Runaway Spent 11 Days in the Subways," *New York Times*, 24 November 2009, www.nytimes.com/2009/11/24/nyregion/24runaway .html?_r=1&pagewanted=print (accessed 26 December 2009).

4. "Franklin Runaway Located with Kentucky Man She Met Online," *Tennessean.com*, 31 March 2009, http://tennessean.mlogic.mobi/news.jsp ?key=226885&rc=ne (accessed 4 January 2010).

5. Federal Bureau of Investigation, "'Innocence Lost' Sting Sixteen-City Sweep Marks Fifth Anniversary," FBI press release, 25 June 2008, www.fbi .gov/news/stories/2008/june/innocencelost_062508 (accessed 5 June 2010).

6. Richard Seven, "Lost, but Not Forgotten," *Seattle Times*, 29 January 2006, www.nampn.org/media/articles/story8.html (accessed 26 December 2009).

7. Ian Urbina, "For Runaways, Sex Buys Survival," *New York Times*, 27 October 2009, www.nytimes.com/2009/10/27/us/27runaways.html (accessed 26 December 2009).

8. Kevin L. Perkins, Assistant Director, FBI, statement before the Senate Judiciary Committee, 2 March 2011, www.fbi.gov/news/testimony/helping -law-enforcement-find-missing-children (accessed 5 June 2011).

9. Heather Hammer, David Finkelhor, and Andrea J. Sedlak, "Runaway/ Thrownaway Children: National Estimates and Characteristics," *NISMART*,

October 2002, www.ncjrs.gov/html/ojjdp/nismart/04/index.html (accessed 22 December 2009).

10. National Runaway Switchboard, "NRS Call Statistics," 2009, www.nrscrisisline.org/news_events/call_stats.html (accessed 3 February 2011).

11. Hammer, et al., "Runaway/Thrownaway Children."

12. Vestena Robbins, Norin Dollard, Beth Jordan Armstrong, Krista Kutash, and Keren S. Vergon, "Mental Health Needs of Poor Suburban and Rural Children and Their Families," *Journal of Loss and Trauma* 13, nos. 2–3 (March 2008), 94–122.

13. Kathy L. Reschke, "Keeping Children Safe from Abduction by Strangers," Family Tapestries, 2002, http://ohioline.osu.edu/flm02/FS17.html (accessed 9 September 2008).

14. Federal Bureau of Investigation, "NCIC Missing Person File," 2008, www.fbi.gov/hq/cjisd/missingpersons.htm (accessed 7 January 2010).

15. Ryan Kath, "Missing Bates Co. Man Gets National Attention," *NBC Action News KSHB-TV 41*, 10 August 2008, www.nbcactionnews.com/news/local/story/Missing-Bates-Co-Man-Gets-National-Attention/5KykwRNs70aIG25ybV2fBQ.cspx (accessed 27 December 2009).

16. "Rancher Vanishes into Thin Air," *America's Most Wanted*, 12 December 2009, www.amw.com/fugitives/case.cfm?id=65213 (accessed 27 December 2009).

17. Eric Pera, "Nurse Matches Man with Identity," *Ledger* (Lakeland, FL), April 2006, www.nampn.org/media/articles/story7.html (accessed 26 December 2009).

18. Pera, "Nurse Matches Man with Identity."

19. Pera, "Nurse Matches Man with Identity."

20. Kim Cobb, "Suburbia Provides Hide-Out in Full Sight," *Houston Chronicle*, 11 June 2005, www.nampn.org/media/articles/story4.html (accessed 6 December 2010).

21. Jane Prendergast, Brenna R. Kelly, and Mike Rutledge, "'Missing' Woman's Mom Is Reaching Out," *Cincinnati Enquirer*, 7 June 2005, www.nampn.org/media/articles/story3.html (accessed 26 December 2009).

22. "Missing Texas Student Found After 7 Years," *FOXNews.com*, 5 June 2005, www.foxnews.com/printer_friendly_story/0,3566,158639,00.html (accessed 11 December 2010).

23. "Missing Texas Student."

24. Cobb, "Suburbia Provides Hide-Out in Full Sight."

25. Federal Bureau of Investigation, "NCIC Missing Person File."

26. Nancy Ritter, "Missing Persons and Unidentified Remains: The Nation's Silent Mass Disaster," *NIJ Journal*, 256, January 2007, www.nij.gov/journals/256/missing-persons.html (accessed 6 June 2011).

27. Ellen Barry, "Alzheimer's Wanderers Stir Concerns," *Boston Globe*, 25 December 1999, A1.

28. Barry, "Alzheimer's Wanderers Stir Concerns."

CHAPTER 2

1. Maira Ansari, "Bullitt County Couple Arrested after Runaway Children Tell of Beating," *Wave 3*, 7 July 2009, www.wave3.com/story/10658571bullitt -county-couple-arrested-after-runaway-children-tell-of-beating?redirected =true (accessed 8 October 2010).

2. Ansari, "Bullitt County Couple Arrested."

3. Tim Padgett, "A Florida Culture-War Circus over Rifqa Bary," *Time*, 24 August 2009, www.time.com/time/nation/article/0,8599,1918228,00.html (accessed 28 October 2010).

4. U.S. Department of Justice, *Sexual Assault of Young Children as Reported to Law Enforcement: Victim, Incident, and Offender Characteristics* (Washington DC: U.S. Government Printing Office, July 2000), 4.

5. Janet Kornblum, "Meet the Child Molester Next Door," *USA Today*, 28 January 2003, www.usatoday.com (accessed 7 May 2005).

6. "Homeless People—Rebecca's Story," *Rebecca's Community*, 2003, www.homeless.org.au/people/rebecca.htm (accessed 25 October 2010).

7. Shauna DeMeritt, "Campus Events Promote 'Sexual Awareness Month,'" *NIC Sentinel*, 18 April 2011, www.nicsentinel.com/news/2011/04/18/Life/ (accessed 6 June 2011).

8. Robert L. Snow, *Sex Crimes Investigation: Catching and Prosecuting the Perpetrators* (New York: Praeger, 2006).

9. Runaway Lives, "On the Other Side of the Streets," 2009, www2 .lv.psu.edu/jkl1/runawaylives/OnTheOtherSideoftheStreets.html (accessed 10 October 2010).

10. Runaway Lives "Just a Kid Myself," 2009, www2.lv.psu.edu/jkl1/ runawaylives/JustaKidMyself.html (accessed 10 October 2010).

11. Runaway Lives, "Running Habit," 2009, www2.lv.psu.edu/jkll/ runawaylives/RunningHabit.html (accessed 10 October 2010).

12. Martha Irvine, "National Runaway Hotline Gets 100,000 Calls a Year," *Pantagraph.com*, 19 July 2008, www.pantagraph.com/news/article_585fda07 -ef38-5e4e-80c6-0e9b215a8201.html (accessed 9 October 2010).

13. "Is There Any Way You Can Help Me?" *Frontline*, Fall 2005, 5.

14. Edith Brady-Lunny, "Runaways Learn Life Lesson at Project Oz," *Pantagraph.com*, 19 July 2008, www.pantagraph.com/news/article_059d116a -d35b-5c95-8037-2c5c3a265542.html (accessed 9 October 2010).

15. Robert Seith, "Runaways," *Connect with Kids*, 3 July 2002, www .connectwithkids.com/tipsheet/2002/79_jul03/runaway.html (accessed 22 December 2009).

16. E. K. Stapleton, "Why Children Sometimes Run Away from Home," *Helium*, 2010, www.helium.com/items/968494-why-children-sometimes -run-away-from-home (accessed 12 October 2010).

17. Tiffany Teasley, "Strong Link Found between Illinois Divorce Rates, Runaway Children," *Medill Reports*, 31 May 2007, http://news.medill .northwestern.edu/chicago/news.aspx?id=37543&print=1 (accessed 9 October 2010).

18. Patricia M. Sullivan and John F. Knutson, "The Prevalence of Disabilities and Maltreatment among Runaway Children," *Child Abuse & Neglect* 24, no. 10 (October 2000), 1275–1288.

19. Iowa Department of Human Rights, "Iowa Criminal and Juvenile Justice Plan, 1997 Update," February 1997, 6–7.

20. A. Jia Son, "Information Packet: Runaway and Homeless Youth," National Resource Center for Foster Care & Permanency Planning, Hunter College, May 2002, 4.

21. Jennifer Shakeel, "Runaways—Why Do Kids Run?" *More4Kids*, 2009, www.more4kids.info/1609/runaways-why-do-kids-run/ (accessed 12 October 2010).

22. James Lehman, "Running Away, Part II," *Empowering Parents*, October 2009, www.empoweringparents.com/article_print.php?id=170 (accessed 15 October 2010).

CHAPTER 3

1. David Altimari, "Why Are They Still Missing?" *Hartford Courant*, 15 April 2001, www.vachss.com/help_text/archive/why_missing1.html (accessed 9 October 2010).

2. Altimari, "Why Are They Still Missing?"

3. David Finkelhor, Heather Hammer, and Andrea J. Sedlak, *National Incidence Studies of Missing, Abducted, Runaway, and Thrownaway Children* (Washington, DC: U.S. Department of Justice, 2002), www.ojjdp.ncjrs.org (accessed 5 November 2009).

4. Kathy L. Reschke, "Keeping Children Safe from Abduction by Strangers," Family Tapestries, 2002, http://ohioline.osu.edu/flm02/FS17.html (accessed 9 September 2008).

5. Rob Schneider, "Pilot in Fatal Crash Called Bitter, Caring," *Indianapolis Star*, 7 March 2007, A-1.

6. Robert L. Snow, *Child Abduction: Prevention, Investigation, and Recovery* (New York: Praeger, 2008).

7. David Finkelhor and Richard Ormrod, "Kidnapping of Juveniles: Patterns from NIBRS," U.S. Department of Justice, Juvenile Justice Bulletin, June 2000.

8. Finkelhor, Hammer, and Sedlak, *National Incidence Studies.*

9. Chris Profitt, "Police Investigate Cyber-Sex Crime Involving Girl, 12," *13 WTHR*, 1 November 2010, www.wthr.com/story/13423115/police -investigate-cyber-sex-crime-involving-12-year-old-girl (accessed 6 June 2011).

10. Katherine M. Brown, Robert D. Keppel, Joseph G. Weis, and Marvin E. Skeen, *Case Management for Missing Children Homicide Investigation* (Olympia, WA: Office of the Attorney General, 2006), www.missingkids .com/en_US/documents/homicide_missing.pdf (accessed 10 March 2011).

CHAPTER 4

1. U.S. Department of Justice, "Hawaii Man Charged with Sex-Trafficking of a Minor over Super Bowl Weekend," press release, 9 February 2010, www .justice.gov/usao/fls/PressReleases/100209-04.html (accessed 10 November 2010).

2. "Hawaii Man Charged with Sex Trafficking at Super Bowl," *Hawaii News Now*, 10 February 2010, www.hawaiinewsnow.com/global/story.asp ?s=11965638 (accessed 10 November 2010).

3. "Hawaii Man Charged."

4. Runaway Lives, "The True Story of My Life," 2009, www2.lv.psu.edu/jkl1/ runawaylives/TrueStoryofMyLife.html (accessed 10 October 2010).

5. Runaway Lives, "Still on the Road," 2009, www2.lv.psu.edu/jkl1/ runawaylives/StillOnTheRoad.html (accessed 10 October 2010).

6. Lynn Zinser and Nate Schweber, "Lawrence Taylor Charged with Rape," *New York Times*, 7 May 2010, B10.

7. "Taylor Charged with Rape, Solicitation," *ESPN*, 7 May 2010, http:// sports.espn.go.com/new-york/nfl/news/story?id=5167613 (accessed 10 November 2010).

8. Ian Urbina, "For Runaways, Sex Buys Survival," *New York Times*, 27 October 2009, www.nytimes.com/2009/10/27/us/27runaways.html (accessed 26 December 2009).

9. "Innocence Lost Initiative Fights Child Trafficking," *Frontline*, Winter 2007, 1.

10. "President's Message," *Frontline*, Winter 2007, 2.

11. Mary Jane Rotheram-Borus, Heino F. L. Meyer-Bahlburg, Cheryl Koopman, Margaret Rosario, Theresa M. Exner, Ronald Henderson, Marjory Matthieu, and Rhoda S. Gruen, "Lifetime Sexual Behaviors among Runaway Males and Females," *Journal of Sex Research* 29, no. 1 (February 1992), 15–29.

12. Federal Bureau of Investigation, "Innocence Lost," www.fbi.gov/about-us/ investigate/vc_majorthefts/cac/innocencelost/ (accessed 12 November 2010).

13. Urbina, "For Runaways, Sex Buys Survival."

14. Susan Skiles Luke, "6 Charged in Ill. Child-Porn Ring," *Boston Globe*, 9 February 2004, www.boston.com/news/nation/articles/2004/02/09/6_charged_ in_ill_child_porn_ ring/?comments=all (accessed 7 June 2011).

15. Ohio Attorney General, "Ohio Runaways At-Risk for Human Trafficking, Report Finds," press release, February 2010.

16. Debra Gwartney, "Good Guys, Bad Guys, and Runaways," *OregonLive. com*, 8 November 2009, www.oregonlive.com/opinion/index.ssf/2009/11/good_ guys_bad_guys_and_runaways.html (accessed 10 November 2010).

17. June R. Wyman, "Drug Abuse among Runaways and Homeless Youths Calls for Focused Outreach Solutions," *NIDA Notes*, May/June 1997, http:// archives.drugabuse.gov/NIDA_Notes/NNVol12N3/Runaway.html (accessed 10 November 2010).

18. Cheryl Koopman, Margaret Rosario, and Mary Jane Rotheram-Borus, "Alcohol and Drug Use and Sexual Behaviors Placing Runaways at Risk for HIV Infection," *Addictive Behaviors* 19, no. 1 (January/February 1994), 95–103.

19. "'Cool Party Mom' Accused of Giving Alcohol to Runaway Teens," *The Denver Channel*, 17 April 2007, www.thedenverchannel.com/news/12310962/ detail.html (accessed 10 November 2010).

20. "'Cool Party Mom' Accused."

21. A. H. Kral, B. E. Molnar, R. E. Booth, and J. K. Watters, "Prevalence of Sexual Risk Behaviour and Substance Use among Runaway and Homeless Adolescents in San Francisco, Denver, and New York City," *International Journal of STD & AIDS* 8, no. 2 (1997), 109–117.

22. Iowa Department of Human Rights, "Iowa Criminal and Juvenile Justice Plan, 1997 Update," February 1997, 7.

23. Runaway Lives, "Personal Stories and Reflections by Runaways and Their Families," 2009, www2.lv.psu.edu/jkl1/runawaylives/ (accessed 13 November 2010).

24. Christine Pelisek, "Raven, Death of a Hollywood Beauty," *LA Weekly News*, 6 May 2010, www.laweekly.com/2010-05-06/news/raven-death-of-a -hollywood-beauty/ (accessed 10 November 2010).

25. Pelisek, "Raven, Death of a Hollywood Beauty."

26. John Asbury, "Man to Die for Killing Teen Runaway Kayla Wood," *Press-Enterprise*, 30 July 2010, www.pe.com/localnews/inland/stories/PE_News_ Local_D_webkayla31.ea5fl8. html (accessed 12 November 2010).

27. "Jury Recommends Death Penalty for Man Who Murdered 16-year-Old Runaway Girl," *Valley News*, 26 April 2010, www.myvalleynews.com/story/47372 (accessed 10 November 2010).

28. Wyman, "Drug Abuse among Runaways."

CHAPTER 5

1. "Teen Runaway Feared in Danger," *KOMO News*, 14 October 2009, www. komonews.com/news/local/64326852.html (accessed 12 October 2010).

2. Bill Christianson, "Runaway Girl Found by Lynnwood Police," *Redmond Reporter*, 4 November 2009, www.pnwlocalnews.com/east_king/red/ news/69176627.html (accessed 10 November 2010).

3. Levi Pulkkinen, "Charge: Seattle Woman Attempted to Use Runaway Kids in 'Escort Service,'" *Seattle PI*, 7 April 2010, www.seattlepi.com/local/418005_charges06.html (accessed 10 November 2010).

4. Greg Sowinski, "Runaway Children and the Coppler Case," *Lima Ohio.com*, 9 May 2009, www.limaohio.com/common/printer/view.php?db=limanews&id=37170 (accessed 9 October 2010).

5. Sowinski, "Runaway Children and the Coppler Case."

6. Deidre Pike, "On the Run," *Las Vegas City Life*, 11 August 2004, www.lasvegascitylife.com/articles/2004/08/11/cover_story/cover.prt (accessed 12 October 2010).

7. Katherine Mieszkowski, "Runaway Daughters," *Salon.com*, 7 March 2009, www.salon.com/life/feature/2009/03/07/live_through_this (accessed 15 October 2010).

8. Phoenix Police Department, "Missing Persons Detail," 2010, www.ci.phoenix.az.us/police/missin1.html (accessed 9 October 2010).

9. "Hanover Missing-Person Case Has Happy Ending," *Richmond Times-Dispatch*, 13 November 2009, www2.timesdispatch.com/news/2009/nov/13/miss13_20091112-222608-ar-26763/ (accessed 14 December 2010).

10. Chris Sikich and Heather Gillers, "Experts: Parents, Kids Must Report Threats," *Indianapolis Star*, 26 March 2011, A5.

11. "Greyhound and National Runaway Switchboard Join Forces to Help Teens Return Home," *Business Wire*, 21 December 1995, http://findarticles.com/p/articles/mi_m0EIN/is_1995_Dec_21/ ai_17913942/ (accessed 10 October 2010).

12. "Runway Runaway: Should Airlines Crack Down on Teens Traveling Alone?" *ABC News*, 21 August 2007, http://abcnews.go.com/GMA/AmericanFamily/story?id=3504782&page=1 (accessed 23 February 2011).

13. "Runway Runaway."

14. Kelly Dedel, *Juvenile Runaways* (Washington, DC: U.S. Government Printing Office, February 2006), 2.

15. Pike, "On the Run."

16. Carolyn B. Maloney, "Maloney Bill Would Improve Reporting of Runaway Children," U.S. Representative Carolyn B. Maloney press release, 23 November 2009, http://maloney.house.gov/index.php?option=content&task=view&id=1980&Itemid=61 (accessed 16 October 2010).

17. U.S. Department of Justice, *Using Agency Records to Find Missing Children: A Guide for Law Enforcement* (Washington, DC: U.S. Government Printing Office, March 1996), 1.

18. Maloney, "Maloney Bill Would Improve Reporting."

19. Julie Carey, "Va. Lawyer Accused of Producing Child Porn," *NBC-Washington.com*, 23 August 2010, www.nbcwashington.com/news/local-beat/Virginia-Lawyer-Accused-of-Producing-Child-Porn-101333809.html (accessed 11 December 2010).

20. Leigh Hearon, Interview by author, 27 February 2011.

21. U.S. Department of Justice, *Using Agency Records*, 13.

22. Robert L. Snow, *Deadly Cults: The Crimes of True Believers* (New York: Praeger, 2003).

23. Maureen Blaha, Interview by author, 27 February 2011.

24. U.S. Department of Education, "Rates of Computer and Internet Use by Children in Nursery School and Students in Kindergarten through Twelfth Grade: 2003," October 2005, http://nces.ed.gov/pubs2005/2005111rev.pdf (accessed 9 February 2009).

25. Max Roll, "Mom Uses Facebook to Help Find Runaway Daughter," Scripps Howard News Service, 10 November 2010, www.scrippsnews.com/content/mom-uses-facebook-help-find-runaway-daughter (accessed 16 November 2010).

26. Linda Thomas, "Missing: Using Social Media to Find a Runaway in Seattle," *MyNorthwest.com*, 8 June 2010, www.mynorthwest.com/?nid =646&sid=328963 (accessed 16 November 2010).

27. "Mineral County Sheriff Statement on Kelsey Ray Return to Her Family," *Clark Fork Chronicle*, 8 June 2010, www.clarkforkchronicle.com/article .php/20100608153147337 (accessed 16 November 2010).

28. Kimberly Barbour, "Henderson Teen Found, Man Arrested for Hiding Her," *News25*, 19 September 2010, www.news25.us/Global/story .asp?S=13181238 (accessed 20 November 2010).

29. Barbour, "Henderson Teen Found."

30. Michael J. Williams, "Lake Elsinore: Outlet Sign Features Missing Teens," *North County Times*, 20 May 2009, www.nctimes.com/news/local/lake-elsinore/article_d4864819-8baf-58ff-b97b-fe8bfdd2caa5.html (accessed 13 October 2010).

31. Williams, "Lake Elsinore."

32. National Center for Missing and Exploited Children, "25 Years: 1984–2009," December 2009, www.missingkids.com/missingkids/servletPageServlet? LanguageCountry=en_US& PageId=244 (accessed 22 December 2009).

33. Encyclopedia of Children's Health, "Running Away," 2005, www .healthofchildren.com/R/Running-Away.html (accessed 15 October 2010).

34. Rod Minott, "Teen Runaways," *PBS*, 14 May 1996, www.pbs.org/ newshour/bb/youth/runaways_5-14.html (accessed 10 October 2010).

35. ICS World, "Runaway and Missing Children," www.icsworld.com/ Private_Investigation_Case_Types/Runaway_and_Missing_Children.aspx (accessed 9 October 2010).

36. Mieszkowski, "Runaway Daughters."

37. Ed Opperman, Interview by author, 12 February 2011.

CHAPTER 6

1. SomeoneIsMissing.com, "Found Safe!" 2007, http://someoneismissing .com/new-hampshire/laura-mackenzie.htm (accessed 19 December 2010).

2. SomeoneIsMissing.com, "Found Safe!"

3. "Disappearance on Website of Missing Maura Murray," *WMUR.com*, 2 September 2006, www.wmur.com/print/9782769/detail.html (accessed 19 December 2010).

4. Tracy Vedder, "What Happened to Darrel Kempf?" *KOMO News*, 26 February 2007, www.komonews.com/news/problemsolvers/6087536.html (accessed 19 December 2010).

5. Tracy Vedder, "Washington Car Dealer Wanted in All 50 States," *KVAL.com*, 31 July 2008, www.kval.com/news/national/26148614.html (accessed 7 December 2010).

6. "Missing Man Found in Grand Rapids," *Fox 17 News*, 27 November 2010, www.fox17online.com/news/fox17-kent-county-police-asking-for-112610,0,7977095.story (accessed 1 February, 2011).

7. Chuck Whitten, "Missing Person Investigation Leads to Suicide Discovery," *KNCO Newstalk Radio*, 25 May 2010, www.knco.com/Local/751848-Missing-Person-Investigation-Leads-Suicide-Discovery.html (accessed 10 December 2010).

8. Sharon Adario, "Former Edison Police Director Brian Collier Dies in Apparent Suicide," *NJ.com*, 27 February 2010, www.nj.com/news/index.ssf/2010/02/former_edison_police_director.html (accessed 13 December 2010).

9. Ohio Intel, "Find Missing Person," www.ohiointel.com/find-missing-person.html (accessed 8 June 2011).

CHAPTER 7

1. Al Baker and Kenny Porpora, "Blind Bronx Man Falls to Death in Elevator Shaft," *New York Times*, 2 May 2009, A18.

2. Baker and Popora, "Blind Bronx Man."

3. Patrick Healy, "L.I. Man Mourned Pair He Is Accused of Killing," *New York Times*, 17 December 2003, www.nytimes.com/2003/12/17/nyregion/li-man-mourned-pair-he-is-accused—of-killing.html (accessed 7 December 2010).

4. "Woman Vanishes at Skyscraper Near Ground Zero," *KVAL.com*, 10 July 2009, www.kval.com/news/national/50472812.html (accessed 7 December 2010).

5. "Woman Vanishes."

6. Hector Castro, "Missing-Person Website Solves Mystery for Family," *Seattle Post-Intelligencer*, 30 May 2005, www.nampn.org/media/articles/story2.html (accessed 26 December 2009).

7. Andrea Cavanaugh, "Missing Persons Haunt Investigators," *LA Daily News*, 1 February 2005, www.thefreelibrary.com/MISSING+PERSONS+HAUNT+INVESTIGATORS-a0128394719 (accessed 8 December 2010).

CHAPTER 8

1. Megan Stromberg, "Young Mother, Lover Still Missing after 40 Years," *Columbus Telegram*, 18 September 2005, http://columbustelegram.com/news/article_08502c0c-770d-536a-a1b2-f4820459eadf.html (accessed 12 December 2010).

2. "Exclusive: Missing Couple Found 40 Years Later," *Action3News.com*, 4 May 2009, www.action3news.com/Global/story.asp?S=10302187 (accessed 11 December 2010).

3. "Exclusive: Missing Couple Found 40 Years Later."

4. Nancy Meersman, "Woman Missing 17 Years Is Found," *New Hampshire Union Leader*, 14 May 2002, www.doenetwork.org/media/news147.html (accessed 8 June 2011).

5. Meersman, "Woman Missing 17 Years Is Found."

6. Barbara Polletta, "Raymond Mystery Solved," *Seacoastonline.com*, 17 May 2002, www.seacoastonline.com/articles/20020517-NEWS-305179917?cid=sitesearch (accessed 8 June 2011).

7. Leigh Hearon, Interview by author, 27 February, 2011.

8. Andrea Cavanaugh, "Missing Persons Haunt Investigators," *LA Daily News*, 1 February 2005, www.thefreelibrary.com/MISSING+PERSONS+HAUNT+INVESTIGATORS-a0128394719 (accessed 8 December 2010).

9. Richard Seven, "Lost, but Not Forgotten," *Seattle Times*, 29 January 2006, www.nampn.org/media/articles/story8.html (accessed 26 December 2009).

10. Phoenix Police Department, "Missing Persons Detail," www.ci.phoenix.az.us/police/missin1.html (accessed 9 October 2010).

11. Sarah Skidmore, "Getting Found within 51 Hours Is Key, Study Finds," *KVAL.com*, 17 July 2007, www.kval.com/news/local/8561357.html (accessed 7 December 2010).

12. Vickie Welborn, "Solved: Man Missing Almost 32 Years Is Identified through DNA Analysis," *Shreveport Times*, 1 March 2010, www.shreveporttimes.com/article/99999999/NEWS0301/108310004/Solved-Man-Missing-Almost-32-Years-Is-Identified-Through-DNA-Analysis (accessed 11 December 2010).

13. "Missing Wilmington Woman Found in Arizona," *WWAY News Channel 3*, 18 March 2009, www.wwaytv3.com/missing_woman_found_arizona/03/2009 (accessed 8 December 2010).

14. Lise Olsen and Lewis Kamb, "Missing-Person Cases Are Routinely Ignored," *Seattle Post Intelligencer*, 18 February 2003, www.seattlepi.com/local/108666_missingday18.shtml (accessed 7 December 2010).

15. Preston Sparks and Timothy Cox, "Missing Persons Usually Found," *The Augusta Chronicle*, 17 November 2008, http://chronicle.augusta.com/stories/2008/11/17/met_ 483813.shtml (accessed 11 December 2010).

16. Lisa Beth Pulitzer, "Thousands of Missing-Persons Cases," *New York Times*, 25 July 1993, www.nytimes.com/1993/07/25/nyregion/thousands-of-missing-persons-cases.html (accessed 11 December 2010).

17. Mesa Police Department, "Missing Persons," www.mesaaz.gov/police/MissingPersons/default.aspx (accessed 8 December 2010).

18. Fox Butterfield, "Missing-Person Cases: A Balancing Act for Police," *New York Times*, 21 July 2001, A10.

19. Dan Prochilo, "Detective Finds Montclair Man Who Had Been Missing for a Month," *NorthJersey.com*, 3 September 2010, www.northjersey.com/news/102158859_Detective_finds_Montclair_man_who_had_been_missing_for_a_month.html (accessed 10 December 2010).

20. Jess Lauren, "Locating Missing People—It Doesn't Have to Be a Daunting Task," *Ezine Articles*, 2009, http://ezinearticles.com/?Locating-Missing-People—It-Doesnt-Have-to-Be-a-Daunting-Task&id=3050851 (accessed 9 December 2010).

21. John Silvester, "In Their Sites," *The Age*, 15 November 2009, www.theage.com.au/technology/technology-news/in-their-sites-20091115-igeu.html (accessed 9 December 2010).

22. "Social Media Drive Interest in Missing-Person Cases," *Richmond Times-Dispatch*, 15 November 2009, www2.timesdispatch.com/news/2009/nov/15/miss15_20091114-221806-ar-25868/ (accessed 9 December 2010).

23. Las Vegas Metropolitan Police Department, "Missing Adults," www.lvmpd.com/bureaus/missing_persons_adults.html (accessed 11 December 2010).

24. "Skiptrace," *Wikipedia*, 9 September 2010, http://en.wikipedia.org/wiki/Skiptrace (accessed 15 October 2010).

25. Leigh Hearon, Interview by author, 27 February 2011.

26. Judd Green, Interview by author, 28 February 2011.

27. Leigh Hearon, Interview by author, 27 February 2011.

28. Carrie Ritchie, "Suspect Ordered to Pay Damages in Disappearance," *Indianapolis Star*, 17 November 2010, B1.

29. National Forensic Science Technology Center, "Families Find Hope with New Missing and Unidentified Persons Website," press release, 10 June 2009.

30. Jeff Martin, "NamUs Helps Solve Missing-Persons Cases," *USA Today*, 10 May 2010, www.usatoday.com/news/nation/2010-05-10-namus_N.htm (accessed 9 December 2010).

31. Maria Glod, "New Path to Restore Identities of Missing," *Washington Post*, 21 July 2009, www.washingtonpost.com/wp-dyn/content/article/2009/07/20/AR2009072003540.html (accessed 26 December 2009).

32. Jerrie Dean, "Note Found in Car of Missing Erick Wales," *Examiner.com*, 27 April 2010, www.examiner.com/headlines-in-san-diego/note-found-car-of-missing-erick-wales (accessed 12 December 2010).

33. "Family Says Missing Man Erick Wales Is Located," *San Diego 6 News*, 15 November 2010, www.sandiego6.com/news/local/story/Family-Says

-Missing-Man-Erick-Wales-is-Located/OYLkpK_2H02kR1Ee1MVNbQ
.cspx (accessed 11 December 2010).

34. "Search Dogs Look for Missing Man," *KIROTV.com*, 19 February 2008, www.kirotv.com/news/15348012/detail.html (accessed 15 January 2011).

35. "Missing Man's Car Found, Friends Say," *KIROTV.com*, 18 February 2008, www.kirotv.com/news/15334301/detail.html (accessed 15 January 2011).

36. "Wife Says Missing SeaTac Man Led Secret Life," *KIROTV.com*, 13 February 2009, www.kirotv.com/news/18712980/detail.html (accessed 15 January 2011).

37. "KIRO 7 Finds Father Who Vanished without a Clue," *KIROTV.com*, 10 February 2010, www.kirotv.com/news/22524605/detail.html (accessed 15 January 2011).

38. Sara Israelsen, "Missing Man May Be Found—21 Years Later," *Deseret News*, 2 August 2007, www.deseretnews.com/article/695197042/Missing-man-may-be-found-21-years-later.html (accessed 11 December 2010).

39. Israelsen, "Missing Man May Be Found."

CHAPTER 9

1. Steve Doughty, "Old People with Dementia Have a Duty to Die and Should Be Pushed towards Death, Says Baroness Warnock," *MailOnline*, 20 September 2008, www.dailymail.co.uk/news/article-1058404/Old-people-dementia-duty-die-pushed-death-says-Baroness-Warnonck.html (accessed 18 January 2011).

2. Martin Beckford, "Baroness Warnock: Dementia Sufferers May Have a 'Duty to Die,'" *Telegraph*, 18 September 2008, www.telegraph.co.uk/news/uknews/2983652/Baroness-Warnock-Dementia-sufferers-may-have-a-duty-to-die.htm (accessed 24 January 2011).

3. Beckford, "Baroness Warnock."

4. Charly Arnolt, Randy Yohe, and Stephanie Schelkun, "Missing Man's Family Speaks Out for the First Time," *WSAZ3*, 16 January 2011, www.wsaz.com/mobi/news?storyid=113001979 (accessed 23 January 2011).

5. Jim Phillips, "After Three Days, Search for Missing Elderly Man Suspended," *AthensNews*, 7 January 2011, www.athensnews.com/ohio/article-32939-after-three-days-search-for-missing-elderly-man-suspended.html (accessed 18 January 2011).

6. "Good Samaritan Finds Missing Westmoreland Woman," *WTAE.com*, 20 November 2009, www,wtae.com/news/21673071/detail.html (accessed 9 June 2011).

7. U.S. Census Bureau, "Sixty-Five Plus in the United States," May 1995, www.census.gov/population/socdemo/statbriefs/agebrief.html (accessed 19 January 2011).

8. U.S. Census Bureau, *The Next Four Decades: The Older Population in the United States: 2010–2050* (Washington, DC: U.S. Department of Commerce, 2010).

9. Kathryn L. Hale et al. "Dementia Overview," *eMedicineHealth*, 2010, www.emedicinehealth.com/dementia_overview/article_em.htm (accessed 18 January 2011).

10. MedicineNet, "Dementia," 2010, www.medicinenet.com/dementia/article.htm (accessed 18 January 2011).

11. Cleveland Clinic, "Types of Dementia," 2009, www.clevelandclinic.org/health/health-info/docs/2300/2340.asp?index=9170 (accessed 18 January 2011).

12. Cleveland Clinic, "Types of Dementia."

13. Bob DeMarco, "Alzheimer's Disease and Wandering," *Alzheimer's Reading Room*, 21 November 2010, www.alzheimersreadingroom.com/2010/11/alzheimers-disease-and-wandering.html (accessed 27 January 2011).

14. Courtney Zubowski, "HPD: Body Found Near Missing Elderly Woman's Car," *KHOU.com*, 9 January 2011, www.khou.com/home/Houston-police-search-for-missing-elderly-woman-113172334.html (accessed 18 January 2011).

15. "Missing Elderly Woman Found Dead in Yard of East Knoxville Home," *WATE.com*, 4 December 2010, www.wate.com/Global/story.asp?S=13617968 (accessed 18 January 2011).

CHAPTER 10

1. "Missing Elderly Woman Found," *Niles (MI) Star*, 11 July 2010, www.nilesstar.com/2010/07/11/missing-elderly-woman-found (accessed 18 January 2011).

2. Kevin Lewis, "Home Break-in Leads to Missing 91-Year-Old Woman," *WNDU.com*, 11 July 2010, www.wndu.com/home/ headlines/98182834.html (accessed 27 January 2011).

3. Maryland State Police, "Search Successful for Missing Elderly Frederick Co. Woman," press release, 16 December 2009, www.mdsp.org/media/press_release_details.asp?identifier=884 (accessed 20 January 2011).

4. MissingPatient.com, "Florence Lorraine Leatherman, 84, Found," 17 December 2009, www.missingpatient.com/dementia_blog/category/missingandfound/maryland/page/2/ (accessed 27 January 2011).

5. MissingPatient.com, "Florence Lorraine Leatherman."

6. Bob DeMarco, "Alzheimer's Disease and Wandering," *Alzheimer's Reading Room*, 21 November 2010, www.alzheimersreadingroom.com/2010/11/alzheimers-disease-and-wandering.html (accessed 27 January 2011).

7. Florida Department of Elder Affairs, "Governor Crist Signs Executive Order Creating 'Silver Alert,'" press release, 8 October 2008.

8. Beth Van Zandt, "Muscatine Authorities Find Missing Elderly Woman at Neighbor's House," *The Muscatine Journal*, 14 January 2010, http:// muscatinejournal.com/news/local/article_01bbfb36-b978-5b6b-b7cf-078f9b 063ald.html (accessed 18 January 2011).

9. "National Silver Alert Program Aids Senior Citizens," *FOP Journal*, April 2010, 7.

10. Eddie Flores, "Missing Elderly Man Goes on 500-Mile Trip across the Valley," *KRGV Channel 5 News*, 15 January 2011, www.krgv.com/news/local/ story/Missing-Elderly-Man-Goes-on-500-Mile-Trip-Across/Jasn4ycMHE ahY9n70w79Pg.cspx (accessed 18 January 2011).

11. Marian Gail Brown, "Blumenthal Wants Silver Alerts for Missing Elderly," *NewsTimes.com*, 31 January 2009, www.newstimes.com/news/article/Blumenthal-wants-Silver-Alerts-for-missing-elderly-105423.php (accessed 18 January 2011).

12. Brown, "Blumenthal Wants Silver Alerts for Missing Elderly."

13. Karen Voyles, "Disoriented Woman Named in Silver Alert Spotted by Convenience Store Clerk," *The Gainesville Sun*, 20 December 2010, www .gainesville.com/article/20101220/ARTICLES/101229965 (accessed 19 January 2011).

14. Cynthia Roldan, "Spike in Missing Elderly, Lack of Awareness Prompts New Silver Alert Campaign," *The Palm Beach Post*, 19 August 2010, www .palmbeachpost.com/news/crime/spike-in-missing-elderly-lack-of-awareness -prompts-869206.html (accessed 18 January 2011).

15. Jen Calantone, "Tracking Device Finds Cape Coral Alzheimer's Patient," *News-Press*, 12 January 2011, B5.

16. Donathan Prater, "Sex Offender Arrested in Car of Missing Elderly Woman after Opelika Attack," *oanow.com*, 17 September 2010, www2.oanow .com/member-center/share-this/print/?content=ar843617 (accessed 18 January 2011).

17. "Deputies Search Remote Area for Missing Elderly Woman," *WFTV Orlando*, 26 October 2010, www.wftv.com/news/25512642/detail.html (accessed 18 January 2011).

Bibliography

Adario, Sharon. "Former Edison Police Director Brian Collier Dies in Apparent Suicide." *NJ.com*, 27 February 2010. www.nj.com/news/index.ssf/2010/02/former_edison_police_director.html (accessed 13 December 2010).

Altimari, David. "Why Are They Still Missing?" *Hartford Courant*, 15 April 2001. www.vachss.com/help_text/archive/why_missing1.html (accessed 9 October 2010).

Ansari, Maira. "Bullet County Couple Arrested after Runaway Children Tell of Beating." *Wave 3*, 7 July 2009. www.wave3.com/story/10658571/bullitt-county-couple-arrested-after-runaway-children-tell-of-beating?redirected=true (accessed 8 October 2010).

Arnolt, Charly, Randy Yohe, and Stephanie Schelkun. "Missing Man's Family Speaks Out for the First Time." *WSAZ3*, 16 January 2011. www.wsaz.com/mobi/news?storyid=113001979 (accessed 23 January 2011).

Asbury, John. "Man to Die for Killing Teen Runaway Kayla Wood." *Press-Enterprise*, 30 July 2010. www.pe.com/localnews/inland/stories/PE_News_Local_D_webkayla31.ea5f18.html (accessed 12 November 2010).

Baker, Al, and Kenny Porpora. "Blind Bronx Man Falls to Death in Elevator Shaft." *New York Times*, 2 May 2009, A18.

Barbour, Kimberly. "Henderson Teen Found, Man Arrested for Hiding Her." *News25*, 19 September 2010. www.news25.us/Global/story.asp?S=13181238 (accessed 20 November 2010).

Barry, Ellen. "Alzheimer's Wanderers Stir Concerns." *Boston Globe*, 25 December 1999, A1.

Beckford, Martin. "Baroness Warnock: Dementia Sufferers May Have a 'Duty to Die.'" *Telegraph*, 18 September 2008. www.telegraph.co.uk/

news/uknews/2983652/Baroness-Warnock-Dementia-sufferers-may-have
-a-duty-to-die.htm (accessed 24 January 2011).

Brady-Lunny, Edith. "Runaways Learn Life Lesson at Project Oz." *Pantagraph.com*, 19 July 2008. www.pantagraph.com/news/article_059d116a
-d35b-5c95-8037-2c5c3a265542. html (accessed 9 October 2010).

Brown, Katherine M., Robert D. Keppel, Joseph G. Weis, and Marvin E. Skeen. "Case Management for Missing Children Homicide Investigation." Olympia, WA: Office of the Attorney General, 2006. www.missingkids .com/en_US/documents/homicide_missing.pdf (accessed 10 March 2011).

Brown, Marian Gail. "Blumenthal Wants Silver Alerts for Missing Elderly." *NewsTimes.com*, 31 January 2009. www.newstimes.com/news/article/ Blumenthal-wants-Silver-Alerts-for-missing-elderly-105423.php (accessed 18 January 2011).

Butterfield, Fox. "Missing-Person Cases: A Balancing Act for Police." *New York Times*, 21 July 2001, A10.

Calantone, Jen. "Tracking Device Finds Cape Coral Alzheimer's Patient." *News-Press*, 12 January 2011, B5.

Carey, Julie. "Va. Lawyer Accused of Producing Child Porn." *NBCWashington.com*, 23 August 2010. www.nbcwashington.com/news/local-beat/ Virginia-Lawyer-Accused-of-Producing-Child-Porn-101333809.html (accessed 11 December 2010).

Castro, Hector. "Missing-Person Website Solves Mystery for Family." *Seattle Post-Intelligencer*, 30 May 2005. www.nampn.org/media/articles/story2 .html (accessed 26 December 2009).

Cavanaugh, Andrea. "Missing Persons Haunt Investigators." *LA Daily News*, 1 February 2005. www.thefreelibrary.com/MISSING+PERSONS+HAUNT+ INVESTIGATORS-a0128394719 (accessed 8 December 2010).

Christianson, Bill. "Runaway Girl Found by Lynnwood Police." *Redmond Reporter*, 4 November 2009. www.pnwlocalnews.com/east_king/red/news/ 69176627.html (accessed 10 November 2010).

Cleveland Clinic. "Types of Dementia." 2009. www.clevelandclinic.org/ health/health-info/docs/2300/2340.asp?index=9170 (accessed 18 January 2011).

Cobb, Kim. "Suburbia Provides Hide-Out in Full Sight." *Houston Chronicle*, 11 June 2005. www.napmn.org/media/articles/story4.html (accessed 6 December 2010).

"'Cool Party Mom' Accused of Giving Alcohol to Runaway Teens." *Denver Channel*, 17 April 2007. www.thedenverchannel.com/news/12310962/ detail.html (accessed 10 November 2010).

Dean, Jerrie. "Note Found in Car of Missing Erick Wales." *Examiner.com*, 27 April 2010. www.examiner.com/headlines-in-san-diego/note-found-car -of-missing-erick-wales (accessed 12 December 2010).

Dedel, Kelly. *Juvenile Runaways*. Washington, DC: U.S. Government Printing Office, February 2006, 2.

DeMarco, Bob. "Alzheimer's Disease and Wandering." *Alzheimer's Reading Room*, 21 November 2010. www.alzheimersreadingroom.com/2010/11/ alzheimers-disease-and-wandering.html (accessed 27 January 2011).

DeMeritt, Shauna. "Campus Events Promote 'Sexual Awareness Month.'" *The NIC Sentinel*, 18 April 2011. www.nicsentinel.com/news/2011/04/18/ Life/ (accessed 6 June 2011).

"Deputies Search Remote Area for Missing Elderly Woman." *WFTV Orlando*, 26 October 2010. www.wftv.com/news/25512642/detail.html (accessed 18 January 2011).

"Disappearance on Website of Missing Maura Murray." *WMUR.com*, 2 September 2006. www.wmur.com/print/9782769/detail.html (accessed 19 December 2010).

Doughty, Steve. "Old People with Dementia Have a Duty to Die and Should Be Pushed towards Death, Says Baroness Warnock." *MailOnline*, 20 December 2008. www.dailymail.co.uk/news/article-1058404/Old-people -dementia-duty-die-pushed-death-says-Baroness-Warnock.html (accessed 18 January 2011).

Encyclopedia of Children's Health. "Running Away." 2005. www.healthof children.com/R/Running-Away.html (accessed 15 October 2010).

"Exclusive: Missing Couple Found 40 Years Later." *Action3News.com*, 4 May 2009. www.action3news.com/Global/story.asp?S=10302187 (accessed 11 December 2010).

"Family Says Missing Man Erick Wales Is Located." *San Diego 6 News*, 15 November 2010. www.sandiego6.com/news/local/story/Family-Says -Missing-Man-Erick-Wales-is-Located/OYLkpK_2H02kR1Ee1MVNbQ .cspx (accessed 11 December 2010).

Federal Bureau of Investigation. "Innocence Lost." www.fbi.gov/about-us/ investigative/vc_majorthefts/cac/innocencelost/ (accessed 12 November 2010).

Federal Bureau of Investigation. "'Innocence Lost' Sting Sixteen-City Sweep Marks Fifth Anniversary." Press release, 26 June 2008. www.fbi.gov/news/ stories/2008/june/innocencelost_062508 (accessed 5 June 2010).

Federal Bureau of Investigation. "NCIC Missing Person File." 2008. www.fbi .gov/hq/cjisd/missingpersons.htm (accessed 7 January 2010).

Finkelhor, David, Heather Hammer, and Andrea J. Sedlak. "National Incidence Studies of Missing, Abducted, Runaway, and Thrownaway Children." U.S. Department of Justice, October 2002. www.ojjdp.ncjrs.org (accessed 5 November 2009).

Finkelhor, David, and Richard Ormrod. "Kidnapping of Juveniles: Patterns from NIBRS." U.S. Department of Justice Juvenile Justice Bulletin, June 2000.

Flores, Eddie. "Missing Elderly Man Goes on 500-Mile Trip Across the Valley." *KRGV Channel 5 News*, 15 January 2011. www.krgv.com/news/local/story/Missing-Elderly-Man-Goes-on-500-Mile-Trip-Across/Jasn4ycMHEahY9n70w 79Pg.cspx (accessed 18 January 2011).

Florida Department of Elder Affairs. "Governor Crist Signs Executive Order Creating 'Silver Alert.'" Press release, 8 October 2008.

"Franklin Runaway Located with Kentucky Man She Met Online." *Tennessean.com*, 31 March 2009. http://tennessean.mlogic.mobi/news.jsp?key=226885&rc=ne (accessed 4 January 2010).

Glod, Maria. "New Path to Restore Identities of Missing." *Washington Post*, 21 July 2009. www.washingtonpost.com/wp-dyn/content/article/2009/07/20/AR2009072003540.html (accessed 26 December 2009).

"Good Samaritan Finds Missing Westmoreland Woman." *WTAE.com*, 20 November 2009. www.wtae.com/news/21673071/detail.html (accessed 9 June 2011).

"Greyhound and National Runaway Switchboard Join Forces to Help Teens Return Home." *Business Wire*, 21 December 1995. http://findarticles.com/p/articles/mi_m0EIN/is_1995_Dec_21/ai_17913942/ (accessed 10 October 2010).

Gwartney, Debra. "Good Guys, Bad Guys, and Runaways." *OregonLive.com*, 8 November 2009. www.oregonlive.com/opinion/index.ssf/2009/11/good_guys_bad_guys_and_runaways.html (accessed 10 November 2010).

Hale, Kathryn L. et al. "Dementia Overview." *eMedicineHealth*, 2010. www.emedicinehealth.com/dementia_overview/article_em.htm (accessed 18 January 2011).

Hammer, Heather, David Finkelhor, and Andrea J. Sedlak. "Runaway/Thrownaway Children: National Estimates and Characteristics." *NISMART*, October 2002. www.ncjrs.gov/html/ojjdp/nismart/04/index/html (accessed 22 December 2009).

"Hanover Missing-Person Case Has Happy Ending." *Richmond Times-Dispatch*, 13 November 2009. www2.timesdispatch.com/news/2009/nov/13/miss13_20091112-222608-ar-26763/ (accessed 14 December 2010).

"Hawaii Man Charged with Sex Trafficking at Super Bowl." *Hawaii News Now*, 10 February 2010. www.hawaiinewsnow.com/global/story.asp?s =11965638 (accessed 10 November 2010).

Healy, Patrick. "L.I. Man Mourned Pair He Is Accused of Killing." *New York Times*, 17 December 2003. www.nytimes.com/2003/12/17/nyregion/ li-man-mourned-pair-he-is-accused-of-killing.html (accessed 7 December 2010).

"Homeless People—Rebecca's Story." *Rebecca's Community*, 2003. www .homeless.org.au/people/rebecca.htm (accessed 25 October 2010).

ICS World. "Runaway and Missing Children." www.icsworld.com/Private _Investigation_Case_Types/Runaway_and_Missing_Children.aspx (accessed 9 October 2010).

"Innocence Lost Initiative Fights Child Trafficking." *Frontline*, Winter 2007, 1.

Iowa Department of Human Rights. "Iowa Criminal and Juvenile Justice Plan, 1997 Update," February 1997, 6–7.

Irvine, Martha. "National Runaway Hotline Gets 100,000 Calls a Year." *Pantagraph.com*, 19 July 2008. www.pantagraph.com/news/article_585 fda-07-ef38-5e4e-80c6-0e9b215a8201.html (accessed 9 October 2010).

Israelsen, Sara. "Missing Man May Be Found—21 Years Later." *Deseret News*, 2 August 2007. www.deseretnews.com/article/695197042/Missing-man -may-be-found-21-years-later.html (accessed 11 December 2010).

"Is There Any Way You Can Help Me?" *Frontline*, Fall 2005, 5.

"Jury Recommends Death Penalty for Man Who Murdered 16-Year-Old Runaway Girl." *Valley News*, 26 April 2010. www.myvalleynews.com/ story/47372 (accessed 10 November 2010).

Kath, Ryan. "Missing Bates Co. Man Gets National Attention." *NBC Action News KSHB-TV 41*, 10 August 2008. www.nbcactionnews.com/ news/local/story/Missing-Bates-Co-Man-Gets-National-Attention/ 5KykwRNs70aIG25ybV2fBQ.cspx (accessed 27 December 2009).

"KIRO 7 Finds Father Who Vanished without a Clue." *KIROTV.com*, 10 February 2010. www.kirotv.com/news/22524605/detail.html (accessed 15 January 2011).

Koopman, Cheryl, Margaret Rosario, and Mary Jane Rotheram-Borus. "Alcohol and Drug Use and Sexual Behaviors Placing Runaways at Risk for HIV Infection." *Addictive Behaviors* 19, no. 1 (January/February 1994): 95–103.

Kornblum, Janet. "Meet the Child Molester Next Door." *USA Today*, 28 January 2003. www.usatoday.com (accessed 7 May 2005).

Kral, A. H., B. E. Molnar, R. E. Booth, and J. K. Watters. "Prevalence of Sexual Risk Behavior and Substance Use among Runaway and Homeless

Adolescents in San Francisco, Denver, and New York City." *International Journal of STD & AIDS* 8, no. 2 (1997): 109–117.

Las Vegas Metropolitan Police Department. "Missing Adults." www .lvmpd.com/bureaus/missing_persons_adults.html (accessed 11 December 2010).

Lauren, Jess. "Locating Missing People—It Doesn't Have to Be a Daunting Task." *Ezine Articles*, 2009. http://ezinearticles.com/?Locating-Missing -People---It-Doesn't_Have-to_Be-a-Daunting-Task&id=3050851 (accessed 9 December 2010).

Lehman, James. "Running Away, Part II." *Empowering Parents*, October 2009. www.empoweringparents.com/article_print.php?id=170 (accessed 15 October 2010).

Lewis, Kevin. "Home Break-in Leads to Missing 91-Year-Old Woman." *WNDU.com*. 11 July 2010. www.wndu.com/home/headlines/98182834 .html (accessed 27 January 2011).

Luke, Susan Skiles. "6 Charged in Ill. Child-Porn Ring." *Boston Globe*, 9 February 2004. www.boston.com/news/nation/articles/2004/02/09/6_charged_ in_ill_child_porn_ring/?comments=all (accessed 7 June 2011).

Maloney, Carolyn B. "Maloney Bill Would Improve Reporting of Runaway Children." U.S. Representative Carolyn B. Maloney press release, 23 November 2009. http://maloney.house.gov/index.php?option=content&task =view&id=1980&Itemid=61 (accessed 16 October 2010).

Martin, Jeff. "NamUs Helps Solve Missing-Persons Cases." *USA Today*, 10 May 2010. www.usatoday.com/news/nation/ 2010-05-10-namus_N.htm (accessed 9 December 2010).

Maryland State Police. "Search Successful for Missing Elderly Frederick Co. Woman." Press release, 16 December 2009. www.mdsp.org/media/ press_release_details.asp?identifier=884 (accessed 20 January 2011).

MedicineNet. "Dementia." 2010. www.medicinenet.com/dementia/article .htm (accessed 18 January 2011).

Meersman, Nancy. "Woman Missing 17 Years Is Found." *New Hampshire Union Leader*, 14 May 2002. www.doenetwork.org/media/news147.html (accessed 8 June 2011).

Mesa Police Department. "Missing Persons." www.mesaaz.gov/police/ MissingPersons/default.aspx (accessed 8 December 2010).

Mieszkowski, Katherine. "Runaway Daughters." *Salon.com*, 7 March 2009. www.salon.com/life/feature/2009/03/07/live_through_this (accessed 15 October 2010).

"Mineral County Sheriff Statement on Kelsey Ray Return to Her Family." *Clark Fork Chronicle*, 8 June 2010. www.clarkforkchronicle.com/article .php/20100608153147337 (accessed 16 November 2010).

Minott, Rod. "Teen Runaways." *PBS*, 14 May 1996. www.pbs.org/newshour/ bb/youth/runaways_5-14.html (accessed 10 October 2010).

"Missing Elderly Woman Found." *Niles (MI) Star*, 11 July 2010. www.niles star.com/2010/07/11/missing-elderly-woman-found (accessed 18 January 2011).

"Missing Elderly Woman Found Dead in Yard of East Knoxville Home." *WATE.com*, 4 December 2010. www.wate.com/Global/story. asp?S=13617968 (accessed 18 January 2011).

"Missing Man Found in Grand Rapids." *Fox 17 News*, 27 November 2010. www.fox17online.com/news/fox17-kent-county-police-asking-for -112610,0,7977095.story (accessed 1 February 2011).

"Missing Man's Car Found, Friends Say." *KIROTV.com*, 18 February 2008. www.kirotv.com/news/15334301/detail.html (accessed 15 January 2011).

MissingPatient.com. "Florence Lorraine Leatherman, 84, Found." 17 December 2009. www.missingpatient.com/dementia_blog/category/missingand found/maryland/page/2/ (accessed 27 January 2011).

"Missing Texas Student Found After 7 Years." *FoxNews.com*, 5 June 2005. www.foxnews.com/printer_friendly_story/0,3566,158639,00.html (accessed 11 December 2010).

"Missing Wilmington Woman Found in Arizona." *WWAY News Channel 3*, 18 March 2009. www.wwaytv3.com/missing_woman_found_arizona/03/2009 (accessed 8 December 2010).

National Center for Missing and Exploited Children. "25 Years: 1984–2009." December 2009. www.missingkids.com/missingkids/servlet/Page ServIet?LanguageCountry=en_US&PageID=244 (accessed 22 December 2009).

National Forensic Science Technology Center. "Families Find Hope with New Missing and Unidentified Persons Website." Press release, 19 June 2009.

National Runaway Switchboard. "NRS Call Statistics." 2009. www.nrscrisis line.org/news_events/call_stats.html (accessed 3 February 2011).

"National Silver Alert Program Aids Senior Citizens." *FOP Journal*, April 2010, 7.

Ohio Attorney General. "Ohio Runaways At-Risk for Human Trafficking, Report Finds." Press release, February 2010.

Ohio Intel. "Find Missing Person." www.ohiointel.com/find-missing-person. html (accessed 8 June 2011).

Olsen, Lise, and Lewis Kamb. "Missing-Person Cases Are Routinely Ignored." *Seattle Post Intelligencer*, 18 February 2003. www.seattlepi.com/ local/108666_missingday18.shtml (accessed 7 December 2010).

Padgett, Tim. "A Florida Culture-War Circus over Rifqa Bary." *Time*, 24 August 2009. www.time.com/time/nation/article/0,8599,1918229,00.html (accessed 28 October 2010).

Pelisek, Christine. "Raven: Death of a Hollywood Beauty." *LA Weekly News*, 6 May 2010. www.laweekly.com/2010-05-06/news/raven-death-of-a -hollywood-beauty/ (accessed 10 November 2010).

Pera, Eric. "Nurse Matches Man with Identity." *Ledger* (Lakeland, FL), April 2006. www.nampn.org/media/articles/story7.html (accessed 26 December 2009).

Perkins, Kevin L. Statement before the Senate Judiciary Committee, 2 March 2011. www.fbi.gov.news/testimony/helping-law-enforcement-find -missing-children (accessed 5 June 2011).

Phillips, Jim. "After Three Days, Search for Missing Elderly Man Suspended." *Athens News*, 7 January 2011. www.athensnews.com/ohio/article -32939-after-three-days-search-for-missing-elderly-man-suspended.html (accessed 18 January 2011).

Phoenix Police Department. "Missing Persons Detail." Phoenix Police Department, 2010. www.ci.phoenix.az.us/police/missin1.html (accessed 9 October 2010).

Pike, Deidre. "On the Run." *Las Vegas City Life*, 11 August 2004. www .lasvegascitylife.com/articles/2004/08/11/cover_story/cover.prt (accessed 12 October 2010).

Polletta, Barbara. "Raymond Mystery Solved." *Seacoastonline.com*, 17 May 2002. www.seacoastonline.com/articles/20020517-NEWS-305179917 ?cid=sitesearch (accessed 8 June 2011).

Prater, Donathan. "Sex Offender Arrested in Car of Missing Elderly Woman after Opelika Attack." *oanow.com*, 17 September 2010. www2.oanow.com/ member-center/share-this/print/?content=ar843617 (accessed 18 January 2011).

Prendergast, Jane, Brenna R. Kelly, and Michael Rutledge. "'Missing' Woman's Mom Is Reaching Out." *Cincinnati Enquirer*, 7 June 2005. www .nampn.org/media/articles/story3.html (accessed 26 December 2010).

"President's Message." *Frontline*, Winter 2007, 2.

Prochilo, Dan. "Detective Finds Montclair Man Who Had Been Missing for a Month." *NorthJersey.com*, 3 September 2010. www.northjersey.com/news/102158859_Detective_finds_Montclair_man_who_had_been_missing_for_a_month. html (accessed 10 December 2010).

Profitt, Chris. "Police Investigate Cyber-Sex Crime Involving Girl, 12." *13 WTHR*, 1 November 2010. www.wthr.com/story/13423115/police-investigate-cyber-sex-crime-involving-12-year-old-girl (accessed 6 June 2001).

Pulitzer, Lisa Beth. "Thousands of Missing-Persons Cases." *New York Times*, 25 July 1993. www.nytimes.com/1993/07/25/nyregion/thousands-of-missing-persons-cases.html (accessed 11 December 2010).

Pulkkinen, Levi. "Charge: Seattle Woman Attempted to Use Runaway Kids in 'Escort Service.'" *Seattle PI*, 7 April 2010. www.seattlepi.com/local/418005_charges06.html (accessed 10 November 2010).

"Rancher Vanishes into Thin Air." *America's Most Wanted*, 12 December 2009. www.amw.com/fugitives/case.cfm?id=65213 (accessed 27 December 2009).

Reschke, Kathy L. "Keeping Children Safe from Abduction by Strangers." *Family Tapestries*, 2002. http://ohioline.osu.edu/flm02/FS17.html (accessed 9 September 2008).

Ritchie, Carrie. "Suspect Ordered to Pay Damages in Disappearance." *Indianapolis Star*, 17 November 2010, B1.

Ritter, Nancy. "Missing Persons and Unidentified Remains: The Nation's Silent Mass Disaster." *NIJ Journal*, no. 256 (January 2007). www.nij.gov/journals/256/missing-persons.html (accessed 6 June 2011).

Robbins, Vestena, Norin Dollard, Beth Jordan Armstrong, Krista Kutash, and Keren S. Vergon. "Mental Health Needs of Poor Suburban and Rural Children and Their Families." *Journal of Loss and Trauma* 13, nos. 2–3 (March 2008): 94–122.

Roldan, Cynthia. "Spike in Missing Elderly, Lack of Awareness Prompts New Silver Alert Campaign." *Palm Beach Post*, 19 August 2010. www.palmbeachpost.com/news/crime/spike-in-missing-elderly-lack-of-awareness-prompts-869206.html (accessed 18 January 2011).

Roll, Max. "Mom Uses Facebook to Help Find Runaway Daughter." *Scripps Howard News Service*, 10 November 2010. www.scrippsnews.com/content/mom-uses-facebook-help-find-runaway-daughter (accessed 16 November 2010).

Rotheram-Borus, Mary Jane, Heino F. L. Meyer-Bahlburg, Cheryl Koopman, Margaret Rosario, Theresa M. Exner, Ronald Henderson, Marjory Matthieu, and Rhoda S. Gruen. "Lifetime Sexual Behaviors among Runaway

Males and Females." *The Journal of Sex Research* 29, no. 1 (February 1992): 15–29.

Runaway Lives. "Personal Stories and Reflections by Runaways and Their Families." 2009. www2.lv.psu.edu/jkll/runawaylives/ (accessed 10 October 2010).

"Runway Runaway: Should Airlines Crack Down on Teens Traveling Alone?" *ABC News*, 21 August 2007. http://abcnews.go.com/GMA/American Family/story?id=3504782&page=1 (accessed 23 February 2011).

Sandoval, Edgar, and Corky Siemaszko. "Missing Boy Francisco Hernandez Jr., 13, Lives in Subway System for 11 Days." *NYDailyNews.com*, 24 November 2009. www.nydailynews.com/ny_local/2009/11/24/2009-11-24_missing_boy_francisco_hernandez_jr_13_lives_in_subway_system_for_11_days.html (accessed 6 January 2010).

Schneider, Rob. "Pilot in Fatal Crash Called Bitter, Caring." *Indianapolis Star*, 7 March 2007, A1.

"Search Dogs Look for Missing Man." *KIROTV.com*, 19 February 2009. www.kirotv.com/news/15348012/detail.html (accessed 15 January 2011).

Seith, Robert. "Runaways." *Connect with Kids*, 3 July 2002. www.connectwith kids.com/tipsheet/2002/79_jul03/ runaway.html (accessed 22 December 2009).

Semple, Kirk. "Runaway Spent 11 Days in the Subways." *New York Times*, 24 November 2009. www.nytimes.com/2009/11/24/nyregion/24runaway .html?_r=1&pagewanted=print (accessed 26 December 2009).

Seven, Richard. "Lost, But Not Forgotten." *Seattle Times*, 29 January 2006. www.nampn.org/media/articles/story8.html (accessed 26 December 2009).

Shakeel, Jennifer. "Runaways—Why Do Kids Run?" *More4Kids*, 2009. www .more4kids.info/1609/runaways-why-do-kids-run/ (accessed 12 October 2010).

Sikich, Chris, and Heather Gillers. "Experts: Parents, Kids Must Report Threats." *Indianapolis Star*, 26 March 2011, A5.

Silvester, John. "In Their Sites." *The Age*, 15 November 2009. www.theage .com.au/technology/technology-news/in-their-sites-20091115-igeu.html (accessed 9 December 2010).

Skidmore, Sarah. "Getting Found within 51 Hours Is Key, Study Finds." *KVAL.com*, 17 July 2007. www.kval.com/news/local/8561357.html (accessed 7 December 2010).

"Skiptrace." *Wikipedia*, 9 September 2010. http://en.wikipedia.org/wiki/Skiptrace (accessed 15 October 2010).

Snow, Robert L. *Child Abduction: Prevention, Investigation, and Recovery.* New York: Praeger, 2008.

Snow, Robert L. *Deadly Cults: The Crimes of True Believers.* New York: Praeger, 2003.

Snow, Robert L. *Sex Crimes Investigation: Catching and Prosecuting the Perpetrators.* New York: Praeger, 2006.

"Social Media Drive Interest in Missing-Person Cases." *Richmond Times-Dispatch*, 15 November 2009. www2.timesdispatch.com/news/2009/nov/15/miss15_20091114-221806-ar-25868/ (accessed 9 December 2010).

SomeoneIsMissing.com. "Found Safe!" 2007. http://someoneismissing.com/new-hampshire/laura-mackenzie.htm (accessed 19 December 2010).

Son, A. Jia. "Information Packet: Runaway and Homeless Youth." National Resource Center for Foster Care & Permanency Planning, Hunter College, May 2002, 4.

Sowinski, Greg. "Runaway Children and the Coppler Case." *LimaOhio.com*, 9 May 2009. www.limaohio.com/common/printer/view.php?db=limanews&id=37170 (accessed 9 October 2010).

Sparks, Preston, and Timothy Cox. "Missing Persons Usually Found." *Augusta Chronicle*, 17 November 2008. http://chronicle.augusta.com/stories/2008/11/17/met_483813.shtml (accessed 11 December 2010).

Stapleton, E.K. "Why Children Sometimes Run Away from Home." *Helium*, 2010. www.helium.com/items/968494-why-children-sometimes-run-away-from-home (accessed 12 October 2010).

Stromberg, Megan. "Young Mother, Lover Still Missing after 40 Years." *Columbus Telegram*, 18 September 2005. http://columbustelegram.com/news/article_08502c0c-770d-536a-a1b2-f4820459eadf.html (accessed 12 December 2010).

Sullivan, Patricia M., and John F. Knutson. "The Prevalence of Disabilities and Maltreatment among Runaway Children." *Child Abuse & Neglect* 24, no. 10 (October 2000): 1275–1288.

"Taylor Charged with Rape, Solicitation." *ESPN*, 7 May 2010. http://sports.espn.go.com/new-york/nfl/news/story?id=5167613 (accessed 10 November 2010).

Teasley, Tiffany. "Strong Link Found between Illinois Divorce Rates, Runaway Children." *Medill Reports*, 31 May 2007. http://news.medill.northwestern.edu/chicago/news.aspx?id=37543&print=1 (accessed 9 October 2010).

"Teen Runaway Feared in Danger." *KOMO News*, 14 October 2009. www.komonews.com/news/local/64326852.html (accessed 12 October 2010).

Thomas, Linda. "Missing: Using Social Media to Find a Runaway in Seattle." *MyNorthwest.com*, 8 June 2010. www.mynorthwest.com/?nid=646&sid =328963 (accessed 16 November 2010).

Urbina, Ian. "For Runaways, Sex Buys Survival." *New York Times*, 27 October 2009. www.nytimes.com/2009/10/27/us/27runaways.html (accessed 26 December 2009).

U.S. Census Bureau. *The Next Four Decades*. Washington, DC: U.S. Department of Commerce, 2010.

U.S. Census Bureau. "Sixty-Five Plus in the United States." May 1995. www .census.gov/population/socdemo/statbriefs/agebrief.html (accessed 19 January 2001).

U.S. Department of Education. "Rates of Computer and Internet Use by Children in Nursery School and Students in Kindergarten through Twelfth Grade: 2003." October 2005. http://nces.ed.gov/pubs2005/2005111rev.pdf (accessed 9 February 2009).

U.S. Department of Justice. "Hawaii Man Charged with Sex-Trafficking of a Minor over Super Bowl Weekend." Press release, 9 February 2010. www .justice.gov/usao/fls/PressReleases/100209-04.html (accessed 10 November 2010).

U.S. Department of Justice. *Sexual Assault of Young Children as Reported to Law Enforcement: Victim, Incident, and Offender Characteristics*. Washington, DC: U.S. Government Printing Office, July 2000, 4.

U.S. Department of Justice. *Using Agency Records to Find Missing Children: A Guide for Law Enforcement*. Washington, DC: U.S. Government Printing Office, 1996, 1.

Van Zandt, Beth. "Muscatine Authorities Find Missing Elderly Woman at Neighbor's House." *Muscatine Journal*, 14 January 2010. http://muscatine journal.com/news/local/article_01bbfb36-b978-5b6b-b7cf-078f9b063al d.html (accessed 19 January 2011).

Vedder, Tracy. "Washington Car Dealer Wanted in All 50 States." *KVAL .com*, 31 July 2008. www.kval.com/news/national/26148614.html (accessed 7 December 2010).

Vedder, Tracy. "What Happened to Darrel Kempf?" *KOMO News*, 26 February 2007. www.komonews.com/news/problemsolvers/6087536.html (accessed 19 December 2010).

Voyles, Karen. "Disoriented Woman Named in Silver Alert Spotted by Convenience Store Clerk." *Gainesville Sun*, 20 December 2010. www .gainesville.com/article/20101220/ARTICLES/101229965 (accessed 19 January 2011).

Welborn, Vickie. "Solved: Man Missing Almost 32 Years Is Identified through DNA Analysis." *Shreveport Times*, 1 March 2010. www.shreveport times.com/article/99999999/NEWS0301/108310004/Solved-Man -Missing-Almost-32-Years-Is-Identified-Through-DNA-Analysis (accessed 11 December 2010).

Whitten, Chuck. "Missing Person Investigation Leads to Suicide Discovery." *KNCO Newstalk Radio*, 25 May 2010. www.knco.com/Local/751848 -Missing-Person-Investigation-Leads-Suicide-Discovery.html (accessed 10 December 2010).

"Wife Says Missing SeaTac Man Led Secret Life." *KIROTV.com*, 13 February 2009. www.kirotv.com/news/18712980/detail.html (accessed 15 January 2011).

Williams, Michael J. "Lake Elsinore: Outlet Sign Features Missing Teens." *North County Times*, 20 May 2009. www.nctimes.com/news/local/lake -elsinore/article_d4864819-8baf-58ff-b97b-fe8bfdd2caa5.html (accessed 13 October 2010).

"Woman Vanishes at Skyscraper Near Ground Zero." *KVAL.com*, 10 July 2009. www.kval.com/news/national/50472812.html (accessed 7 December 2010).

Wyman, June R. "Drug Abuse among Runaways and Homeless Youths Calls for Focused Outreach Solutions." NIDA *Notes*, May/June 1997. http:// archives.drugabuse.gov/NIDA_Notes/NNVol12N3/Runaway.html (accessed 10 November 2010).

Zinser, Lynn, and Nate Schweber. "Lawrence Taylor Charged with Rape." *New York Times*, 7 May 2010, B10.

Zubowski, Courtney. "HPD: Body Found Near Missing Elderly Woman's Car." *KHOU.com*, 9 January 2011. www.khou.com/home/Houston-police -search-for-missing-elderly-woman-113172334.html (accessed 18 January 2011).

Index